Warrior • 35

English Medieval
Knight 1400–1500

Christopher Gravett • Illustrated by Graham Turner

First published in Great Britain in 2001 by Osprey Publishing,
Midland House, West Way, Botley, Oxford OX2 0PH, UK
44-02 23rd St, Suite 219, Long Island City, NY 11101, USA
Email: info@ospreypublishing.com

Transferred to digital print on demand 2010

First published 2001
8th impression 2009

Printed and bound in Great Britain

A CIP catalogue record for this book is available from the British Library

ISBN: 978 1 84176 146 6

Editorial by Marcus Cowper
Design by Ken Vail Graphic Design, Cambridge, UK
Index by Alan Rutter
Originated by Magnet Harlequin, Uxbridge, UK
Typeset in Helvetica Neue and ITC New Baskerville

Dedication
To Jane and Joanna, both now heartily sick of knighthood but not of chivalry.

Acknowledgements
My grateful thanks to Terry Jones for discussions on the knight from the *Ellesmere Chaucer*. Guy Wilson, Master of the Armouries,
read the manuscript and made a number of helpful suggestions. Many thanks also to Claude Blair, Simon Metcalf, and to
Thom Richardson and Karen Watts of the Royal Armouries, Leeds, for advice on armour details. Thanks also to Stephen Howe
of the Armouries for photographic assistance, and to Graham Turner and Mark Duffy for help with photographs of effigies.

Editor's note
All emboldened terms in the text are featured in the glossary on page 55.

Artist's note
Readers may care to note that the original paintings from which the colour plates in this book were prepared are available for
private sale. All reproduction copyright whatsoever is retained by the Publishers. All enquiries should be addressed to:

Graham Turner
PO Box 568
Aylesbury
Buckinghamshire
HP17 8ZX
UK

www.studio88.co.uk

The Publishers regret that they can enter into no correspondence upon this matter.

Front cover
The Chronicle of England by Jean de Waurin, late 15th century.
(By permission of the British Library, MS. Roy - 14. E, 201v.)

FOR A CATALOGUE OF ALL BOOKS PUBLISHED BY
OSPREY MILITARY AND AVIATION PLEASE CONTACT:

Osprey Direct, c/o Random House Distribution Center,
400 Hahn Road, Westminster, MD 21157
Email: uscustomerservice@ospreypublishing.com

Osprey Direct, The Book Service Ltd, Distribution Centre,
Colchester Road, Frating Green, Colchester, Essex, CO7 7DW
Email: customerservice@ospreypublishing.com

www.ospreypublishing.com

CONTENTS

ENGLISH MEDIEVAL KNIGHT 1400–1500

INTRODUCTION

The knight in shining full plate armour appeared in the 15th century. As such he became the stuff of medieval legend, of 19th-century romance and, more recently, of television and film. The image of the warrior clad in steel plates is always more impressive than that of his predecessor in armour of mail rings. The great boost to medieval stories given by the contemporary Thomas Malory's tales of King Arthur meant that such sub-Roman warriors were now often identified with 15th-century knights. However, behind the light of Galahad's shining goodness, the real knights of the day could present a varied tapestry of emotions. Many were loyal and true to their king and their followers, well bred and well mannered. Others were self-seekers or social climbers, ruthlessly changing sides for personal gain or preservation. Long campaigns abroad and lethal factional fighting at home could breed hard-bitten men and cultured thugs; even gentlemen could be noted for their sadistic ways. War was hard and knights fought hand to hand. Time has sometimes softened our perspective of their world and painted too rosy a picture.

The 15th century was a time of change for knighthood. Knights no longer fought for their lord in return for land, since the feudal summons had long before given way to a system of contracts. Moreover, many now preferred the lifestyle of the landowner, man-about-town and parliamentary representative, likewise many rich burgesses were now obtaining the rank of knight. Some knights spoke English, French and Latin. At court Sir John Paston amused himself by borrowing Ovid's *De Arte Amandi* ('Art of Love') and was advised to look at the same author's *De Remedio* (Ovid's *Remedio Amoris*, 'Remedies of Love') unless he was going to spend time 'courting' a certain lady.

Great lords, however, still recognised their special role in the order of things. In time of war it was their duty, the reason behind their privileges, to lead from the front. England began the century still embroiled in the Hundred Years War with France, as she had been since 1337. Interspersed with sporadic bouts of peace, the contention for the French crown had begun under Edward III. Despite resounding victories for English armies at Crécy and Poitiers, the French had not been overcome, while the terrible ravages of the Black Death in 1380 had wiped out perhaps a third of the population in England alone.

The Knight, as depicted in the early 15th-century *Ellesmere Chaucer*. He wears a vertically quilted jupon with unusual bagpipe sleeves, which Terry Jones has suggested may have been widened latterly. The four straps at neck and shoulders may have been for securing an external breastplate, or perhaps for tying down the edges of a mail aventail. Note the brand on the horse's rump. (Huntington Library)

The battle of Poitiers (1356) illuminated in the early 15th century. The basinets are now fitted with rounded visors. Few shields are carried and these are convex. Note the lance resting in the cutout. (By permission of the British Library, MS Cotton Nero E II pt 2, f.152v)

As the new century opened under Henry IV, an uneasy peace still held. With the coming of his son, Henry V, in 1412, a new war loomed as the king sought foreign adventure to divert attention from problems at home. His dramatic victory at Agincourt in 1415 solved little, and it was the hard sieges of the following years that really wore down his enemies. Just as it seemed that Henry might unite the two crowns, he died of dysentery in 1422, leaving the throne to a young child, Henry VI. Despite surviving until 1460, Henry would see English pretensions crushed by French insurgence assisted by Joan of Arc, until only Calais remained by 1453.

At home, King Henry, of the house of Lancaster, faced rising opposition to his poor government from the descendants of Edmund of York, one of Edward III's sons. This heralded the civil wars known as the Wars of the Roses. These dynastic struggles, which owed nothing to the modern geographical counties of Yorkshire and Lancashire, would bear witness to some of the bloodiest fighting ever seen in England. The Yorkist Edward IV would seize the crown, lose it and retake it; his son, Edward V, would disappear in the Tower of London; and his brother, Richard III, would die at Bosworth striving to destroy the invading Lancastrian, Henry Tudor. From 1485 the wars were effectively over and England was ruled by a new dynasty.

This French illustration of the poems of Christine de Pisan (*c.*1410) explodes the myth that knights could not mount their horses unaided and without a crane. It shows a knight in full plate armour, with perhaps a complete mail coat beneath, about to climb into his saddle. (By permission of the British Library, MS Harley 4431, f.135)

TRAINING

A boy from a noble household might begin his training for knighthood when only seven years old, though sometimes slightly later. He was often sent to another household, usually that of a relative such as a maternal uncle; sons from great families might arrive at the royal court. He was taught manners and courtesy, how to sing and dance, to serve ladies and make pleasant company. He would learn to groom horses and begin the arduous tasks of becoming familiar with, and looking after, weapons and armour. His master's harness might be stored in cupboards; it had to be kept clean and free of rust (olive oil was best for this), the sliding and pivoting rivets had to be serviceable, leather straps must not be frayed. This training went on for several years until he was 14 or thereabouts. He now became an esquire to a knight, unless proven unsuitable, when he might be packed off to the church. As an esquire, he was increasingly ordered to train with weapons, sometimes of double weight to develop his muscles. Caxton's translation of Christine de Pisan in 1489 says:

'The knyght or men of armes is to be chosen that from the tyme of his youthe hath lerned the trauayllis of armes and the maners of bataille.'

Though many read these military treatises, experience in war was the best way to learn. The esquire rode with the knights in the hunt, and was taught to recognise the different hunting calls and how to correctly dismember a kill. He might learn to use a longbow or crossbow but only for the hunting field; it was not part of his duty to employ such weapons in battle. Hunting also increased riding skills, though horses were not expected to jump fences, and much land was open country or open fields. The youth was also required to follow his master into battle to pull him out of the press if wounded, or remount him if unhorsed. Standards of education were higher than in previous centuries, and the esquire might be taught by a priest or chaplain to read and write Latin or French.

The ceremony of knighting took place when the young man was some-where between about 18 and 21 years old. This was often an excuse for elab-orate displays of feasting and tournaments, and the richer the candidate's circle, the more imposing the ceremony. A well-bred youth might be knighted by the king himself, and on occasion boys were

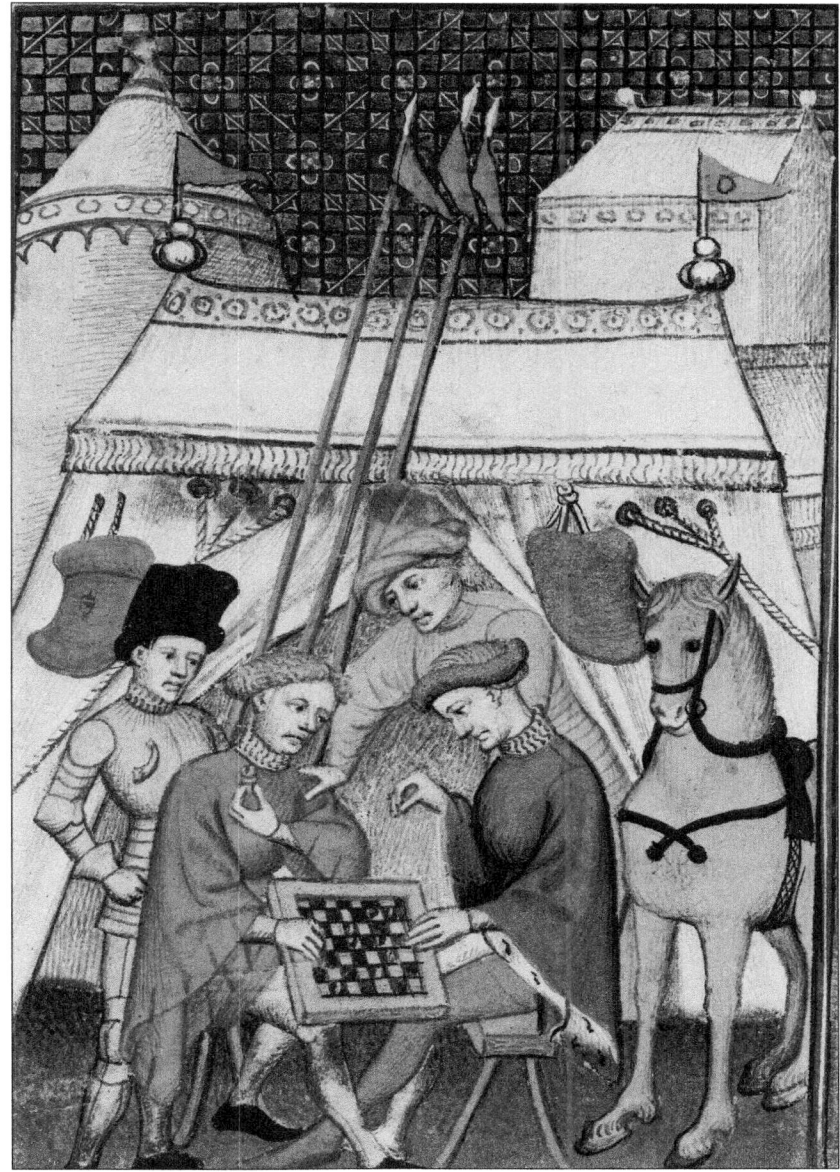

Knights play chess to while away the time during a siege, from a French version of the early 15th-century poems of Christine de Pisan. (By permission of the British Library, MS Harley 4431, f.133r)

knighted before a battle, or sometimes after it for conspicuous service. As a knight he still had to continue his exercises. He would cut at the wooden post or pell, test himself against opponents in the courtyard, or ride against the quintain (a dummy carved on a wooden post). The latter was sometimes equipped with a pivoting top half where a shield was balanced by an arm with a weight suspended from it. A strike against the shield swung the weighted arm to deliver a sound buffet to anyone galloping past too slowly, or to any knight failing to hit the shield squarely. Some might try to catch a suspended ring with the point of the lance, a feat requiring good co-ordination and a steady arm.

By mid-century many nobles were increasingly looking to law or some other peaceful occupation, something railed against by William Worcester in his *Boke of Noblesse*, written at this time. With fewer knights to call upon, advice on warfare had to be sought from veteran captains of the French wars. Training of ordinary soldiers soon came to reflect the different ideas of individual captains in particular areas.

ARMS, ARMOUR AND HORSES

Armour

By the opening years of the 15th century steel plates covered the knight's entire body. The main body protection the previous century had been the coat of plates, or 'plates', in which plates were riveted inside (or occasionally outside) a canvas covering. This was then faced with a richer material such as velvet or even leather, with the rivet heads visible on the outside. The heads were often tinned or gilded and might be of foliate form to enhance the effect.

Plates were usually arranged as horizontal hoops but many had a breast defence of two plates or even a single breastplate. The coat was put on like a poncho and fastened at the back, though a number were side fastening and closed additionally at one or both shoulders.

Many knights now wore 'plates' with an external breastplate and a **fauld** of steel hoops below. Beneath the 'plates' was a long-sleeved mail coat, consisting of thousands of interlinked and individually riveted iron

The early 15th-century Dunstable Swan jewel, found on the site of Dunstable Priory in Bedfordshire. This is the only surviving example of a white enamelled badge in the form of a chained animal. The badge came into the House of Lancaster after the marriage of Henry of Lancaster to Mary de Bohun, whose family was one of those claiming descent from the legendary Swan Knight. (By courtesy of the Trustees of the British Museum, M&LA, 1966, 7–3, 1)

rings. Such coats were usually slightly longer than the 'plates' and might now be provided with an upstanding collar made from thicker rings to provide stiffness. A padded **aketon** was worn beneath to help absorb the shock of a blow, this was necessary because mail was flexible and would yield when struck, even if the links were not torn.

By about 1425, knights increasingly replaced the coat of plates with armour which was attached by **points** (laces, often red) directly to an arming doublet, a padded coat provided with gussets of mail covering the armpit and inner arm. The Hastings manuscript of about 1485 (*How a man schall be armyd at his ese when he schal fighte on foote*) said that points were to be of fine waxed twine such as that used to make crossbow strings, and each would be fitted over the end with a brass 'aiglet' or metal point. Some might be made from buckskin, which is tough and stretchy. A few knights still wore the full mail coat underneath, with elbow-length sleeves over the plates of the upper arm, well into mid-century, a practice more common in Italy.

Arming a knight in alwite armour

A knight was always armed from the feet upwards. Before putting on his armour he donned his leggings, often of woven wool. The Hastings manuscript of about 1485 mentions hose of 'stamyn sengill' (worsted cloth apparently made in Norfolk). On his feet he wore shoes designed to prevent skidding, described in detail:

'Also a payre of shone [shoes] of thikke Cordwene and they muste be frette [fretted] with smal whipcorde thre knottis up on a corde and thre cordis muste be faste swoid [sewn] on to the hele of the shoo and fyne cordis in the mydill of the soole of the same shoo and that ther be betwene the frettis of the hele and the frettis of the mydill of the shoo the space of three fvngris.'

According to the Hastings manuscript no shirt was worn under the fustian arming doublet, which was lined with satin. The question arises as to how the hose were secured, since in mid-century they reached only to the hips,

and even later, when they were higher, they were still anchored with **points** through the civilian doublet. Since it is unlikely that a civilian doublet was worn beneath (also contradicting the Hastings description) it must be supposed that the arming doublet was at this time provided with pairs of eyelet holes near the lower edge. It was practical to leave undone the back pairs, since even in civilian life bending forward violently could cause them to break. The arming doublet would be laced down the front with similar pairs of points passing through pairs of holes cut in the doublet. The Hastings manuscript mentions the doublet as cut full of holes, which may refer to the holes pierced through it for the points; it might also mean it was full of small bound holes, to aid ventilation, though surviving jackets of this form are not arming doublets.

Mail gussets were sewn to the doublet, as described in the Hastings manuscript, though 16th-century illustrations also depict use of points. From the Hastings manuscript we learn that a thin blanket ('shorte bulwerkis') was wrapped around the knees to prevent chafing from the plates. Around the neck a mail upstanding collar was added. This is sometimes thought to have been attached to the collar of the arming doublet, but most detailed effigies show no front fastening, suggesting that the mail collar is a separate item fastened at the back, a more secure method despite the necessity for some assistance when putting it on.

Except for the sole, the foot was covered by a **sabaton**, made from a number of overlapping **lames** connected each side by rivets on which they pivoted. The sabaton was hinged on the outer side of the foot under the ankle, it was closed on the inner side with a strap and buckle. The foot could be slipped through a leather stirrup running under the sole, and might be further secured by points at the top of the shoe, which were laced through holes in the top of the sabaton. If mail sabatons in the Italian style were worn (rare in England) then the edges would be held by straps and the top tied through the shoe; the mail was secured to the **greave** through numerous holes in the lower edge. Greaves were hinged on the outer side but closed by straps and buckles on the inner side, where they were less likely to be cut. They were usually attached to the sabaton by pairs of points.

The **poleyn** and **cuisse** (knee and thigh armour) were added as one item. The upper end of the greave had a turning pin which fitted through a hole in the lower plate of the poleyn, whilst the latter's main plate and the cuisse were held by straps behind the knee and thigh respectively. In order to hold the cuisse against the leg and help support it, a leather tab, riveted to its top edge and pierced with holes, was secured to the lower part of the arming doublet by a pair of points hanging from a similar pair of holes in the doublet. Both legs were armoured in the same fashion.

A mail skirt, to protect the genitals and allow a man to sit down easily, was tied round the waist, perhaps supported by further points along the top edge. For foot combat in war or tournament, a pair of mail pants might be substituted, in which the gusset between the legs was tied in front, however this would be too uncomfortable for use in riding.

The breastplate had the **fauld** attached by internal leathers and, from about 1430, the lower plate was divided in two and hung from straps, becoming known as **tassets**, which gradually lengthened. The

Arming sword of the early 15th century, found in the Triforium of Westminster Abbey in 1869, perhaps from the tomb of Henry V. It could have been used for cutting and thrusting. (Copyright: Dean and Chapter of Westminster)

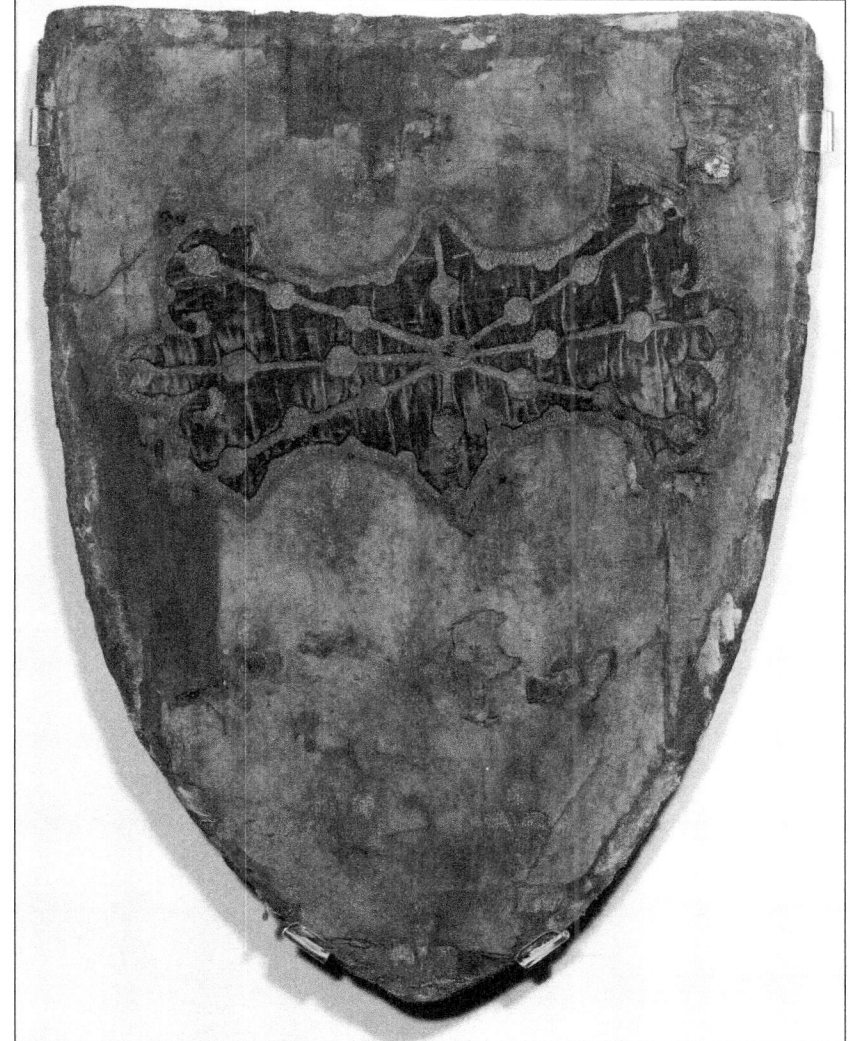

backplate had a **culet** (skirt) form which usually hung a single plate, the **rump-guard**. The **cuirass** could sometimes be donned in one piece if the pins of the fauld only were removed, allowing the breast and back to pivot on their pins. The whole was closed on the wearer's right side by straps and buckles, and by straps over the shoulders. The tassets would probably be already suspended.

The **vambrace** consisted of a gutter-shaped upper arm defence (the 'upper cannon'), a cup-shaped **couter** at the elbow, and a two-part tube (the 'lower cannon') enclosing the forearm. It was simply slid up the arm in one piece, the top edge of the upper cannon being provided with a leather tab for a pair of points at the shoulder of the doublet. The lower cannon was hinged for access and shut with a strap. By about 1430 the upper cannons almost enclosed the upper arm. On Italian armours at this time, asymmetrical reinforcing plates were attached to couter wings and **pauldrons** but west European forms often had separate couters in the German fashion, which necessitated points at the elbows also, for attaching them. The lower cannon probably attached to the lower end of the upper cannon by laces, though the exact method of this fixture is not known for certain.

The shoulder was protected in the first half of the century by a laminated **spaudler** secured by points through holes at the top of one of the plates, and a strap and buckle under the arm. Often a pair of 'besagews' guarded the armpits, being hung from the spaudler or laced on. Besagews were usually circular and sometimes drawn out at the centre to a short spike. By 1440 **pauldrons**, shoulder-defences which overlapped the chest and back, were common, being attached like spaudlers. **Gauntlets** had flared cuffs, and the knuckles might be furnished with 'gadlings', raised pyramids or spikes of steel. By about 1440 mitten gauntlets were replacing those with fingers. The sword was now belted on the left side, and possibly a dagger on the right. The gauntlets might be buttoned over the sword hilt. If the knight was to ride, his spurs were buckled on.

Helmets

The helmet was the last item to be put on. In 1400 most knights wore the **basinet**, an open-faced conical helmet to which was attached a removable mail neck-defence called an **aventail**. The top edge was stitched to a leather strip pierced by slits that fitted over staples on the

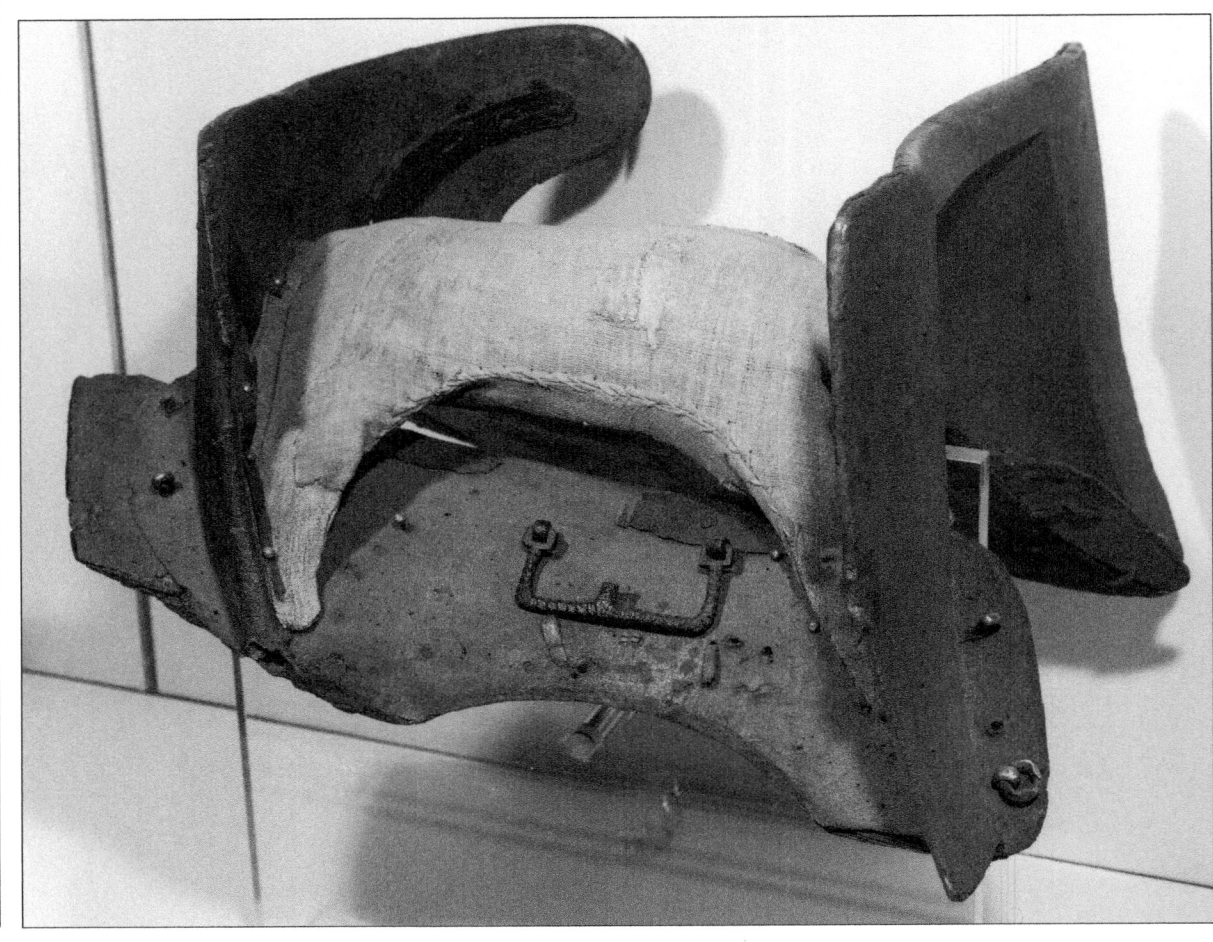

The war saddle used at the funeral of Henry V. Its canvas seat, stuffed with hay, was raised 5 ins (12 cm) off the horse's back. Canvas is glued over all the wooden surfaces, but the blue velvet cover, powdered with fleurs-de-lys, has gone. Above the remains of the double girth is a rectangular ring for the stirrup leather. A staple on the cantle was for the crupper housing, one each side at the front for the peytral housings, but the purpose of the ring is not certain. (Copyright: Dean and Chapter of Westminster)

lower edge of the helmet, being secured by a cord. The visor could usually be detached by withdrawing a pin each side, a pointed form being common until about 1410. By about 1420 the great basinet was increasingly seen, with its attached plate neck-guard called a **gorget**. The front plate often pivoted for access, and had a chin defence (**bevor**) pivoted inside or sometimes attached to it. A more rounded visor was now usual. The whole was usually strapped down to the breast- and back-plates.

By the 1440s the **sallet** and occasionally the **armet** had begun to replace the basinet. The armet opened out at the sides to facilitate placing it over the head, the cheek-pieces being fastened together at the chin by a turning pin. The visor then closed over their upper edges. Further protection might be afforded by a **wrapper**, a frontal plate shaped like a ship's prow and with gorget plates below, which fitted the lower part of the helmet and was secured at the rear by a strap and buckle. The far more popular sallet was sometimes accompanied by a bevor with gorget plates, strapped around the neck and laced through holes in the gorget plate to the breastplate, though rich examples might use a staple instead. The sallet was then secured with a leather chin strap. Most helmets had a leather or canvas lining-band riveted inside, to which was stitched a cloth lining stuffed with hay, horsehair, wool or tow, and often cut into scallops at the top, which could be adjusted by a draw string. Otherwise a lining was glued inside. Other pieces of armour were often also lined. Occasionally a padded arming cap was still worn, tied under the chin.

Shields

Shields were rarely used, except perhaps by cavalry, largely being relegated to the tournament. Typical examples were made from wood, which was faced with leather and sometimes lined with parchment or cloth.

Wearing armour

All this equipment could be put on very quickly if necessary. Once the undergarments were in place, two attendants could arm a knight from head to toe (*cap-à-pie*) if necessary in about five to ten minutes, and remove it in less time still. A complete war harness weighed only about 45–55 lbs (25–35 kg), the weight spread all over

The brass of Sir Giles Daubeney (died 1446) in South Petherton, Somerset. He wears alwite armour with a deep skirt (fauld). Also visible are a great basinet, quadrilateral besagews and shell-winged couters. Note the diagonal sword belt and the dagger, presumably riveted to the fauld. His jousting helm crest is a holly bush out of a wreath of roses.

A knight, depicted in the northern English *Desert of Religion* of the second quarter of the 15th century. His sleeves hang outside the vambraces. The strange staff weapon has a long axe-head with three flukes and a spike, but a cross-bar to stop enemy weapons sliding down the shaft. (By permission of the British Library, MS Cotton Faustina B VI, f.1)

the body, and less than a modern infantryman carries in his backpack. A fit man could run, lie down or mount his horse with ease. There was no need for mechanical aids such as cranes, a later myth which has clung tenaciously largely thanks to misguided films.

It was easy enough to move in full armour; some could (and still do) turn cartwheels, or vault into the saddle. The greatest drawback was the lack of ventilation. The body's heat could not escape easily and the wearer soon got hot, especially when the helmet was in place, since much heat is lost from the head. Some died in the press of battle from suffocation, as did Henry V's brother, the Duke of York, pulled from the crush of bodies at Agincourt (in October) without a scratch. In summer sunshine the metal became hot to touch, in winter it was cold to the touch but hot inside.

The metals used to make armour ranged from iron to impure mild steel containing slag, which could not be removed by the processes available. However, it could turn a sword and was designed to make a weapon point skid off. A v-shaped stop-rib below the neck was welded on to guide a point to right or left of the throat and so away. Ribs were also added at certain other points, such as the pauldron.

Wealthy men might purchase harness from the top armourers of northern Italy or south Germany (Augsburg, Nuremberg or Landshut). A knight of average means might buy a workaday Milanese armour, brought back by merchant ships on return journeys. Sir John Cressy bought such a harness in 1441, costing £8 6s 8d, while armour for a

squire cost from £5 to £6 16s 8d. Wills and inventories show that armours from Lombardy were popular. Pictorial evidence suggests that much English armour was of the style worn in England, France and the Low Countries. Some of this may have been Italian export armour, designed in the style of the area where the armourers wished to make a sale. However, much was probably often purchased from merchant armourers, who offered the relevant parts to make up an armour, which they were sufficiently skilled to adjust to fit the individual purchaser. Armour that does not fit properly is very uncomfortable, especially over the ankle bones. In 1473 Sir John Paston, then with the Calais garrison, negotiated with an armourer in Bruges for a harness, and in January 1475 mentions riding into Flanders to get horses and armour.

The construction of Raglan Castle in Gwent was begun by Sir William ap Thomas in about 1430 and carried on by his son, Sir William Herbert, later earl of Pembroke, until executed in 1469.

Weapons

The main knightly weapon was the sword, with those from Cologne, Milan and Savoy being popular. At the beginning of the century some swords tapered to an acute point, with a blade of flattened diamond-section for stiffness; others had a broader blade that tapered more acutely nearer the point but with edges sharp enough to cut. During the second quarter of the century, a form of blade appeared that was flat in section but which had an upstanding mid-rib. A few broad-bladed weapons had two short fullers (channels) near the cross-guard, with a short single one below, and were probably Italian imports. Some swords were heavy, perhaps 5 lbs (2.2 kg) or more, and some over 50 ins (1.2 m) long, designed as thrusting weapons to combat plate armour. Long, narrow blades tended to have a long grip, to help balance them,

The brass of William Wadham (died 1451), probably made between 1444 and 1450. He wears a great basinet, pauldrons and reinforced couters. The lowest lame of the fauld now becomes separate tassets.

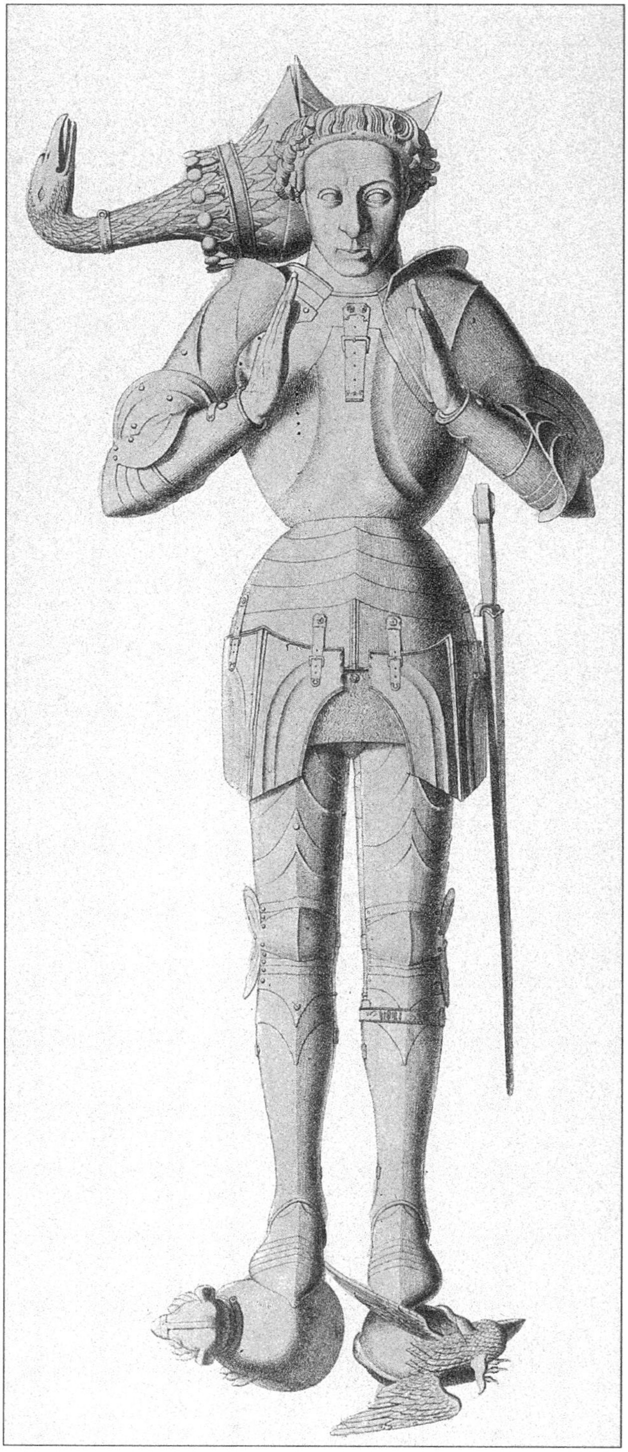

The latten effigy of Richard Beauchamp, Earl of Warwick, at Warwick, made in about 1450, shows him wearing a Milanese armour. His frog-mouthed jousting helm lies surmounted by his swan crest, lays beneath his head.

Sir John Fastolf began the construction of the brick castle at Caister in Norfolk in 1432. The very tall tower set in one corner is the donjon, with fireplaces on each floor except the topmost for the use of Sir John, and with a machicolated parapet and gunports. Caister appears to have repelled a French raid in 1458, when 'many gonnes [sic]' were fired.

and an elongated pommel like a 'scent-bottle'. Larger hand-and-a-half swords were also known as **bastard swords** or 'swords of war'. Many swords had a metal flap on the cross-guard over the blade, which fitted over the scabbard to stop water penetration.

The front section of the blade was sometimes left blunt, since men tended to hook their finger over it; this section was called the 'ricasso'. Some continental sword hilts developed a loop to guard the forefinger, a second loop then appeared to the rear cross-guard. Swords also, on occasion, had a ring on the side of the guard. The design of such guards continued to develop throughout the 15th century, and some incorporated a knuckle guard, although such models were rare in England until the 1500s.

Scabbards were of wood covered in leather, often dyed and sometimes decorated with metal mounts down their length. **Locket** and **chape** (mouth and tip of the scabbard) might be gilded, pierced or set with precious stones. Slits near the top of the scabbard were sometimes made to accommodate a small eating knife and steel for sharpening or a **bodkin**. Jewelled sword belts, often of metal plaques, were worn on the hip (sometimes secured to the armour) until mid-century, but by 1415 diagonal belts had become popular. In mid-century the rear of such belts were forked, the lower part being attached to the scabbard about 12 ins (30 cm) from the mouth, moving it back from the wearer's feet and putting the hilt at a better angle. Occasionally a metal or leather loop was riveted to the fauld to support the scabbard instead of a belt; a dagger might be similarly worn on the right side.

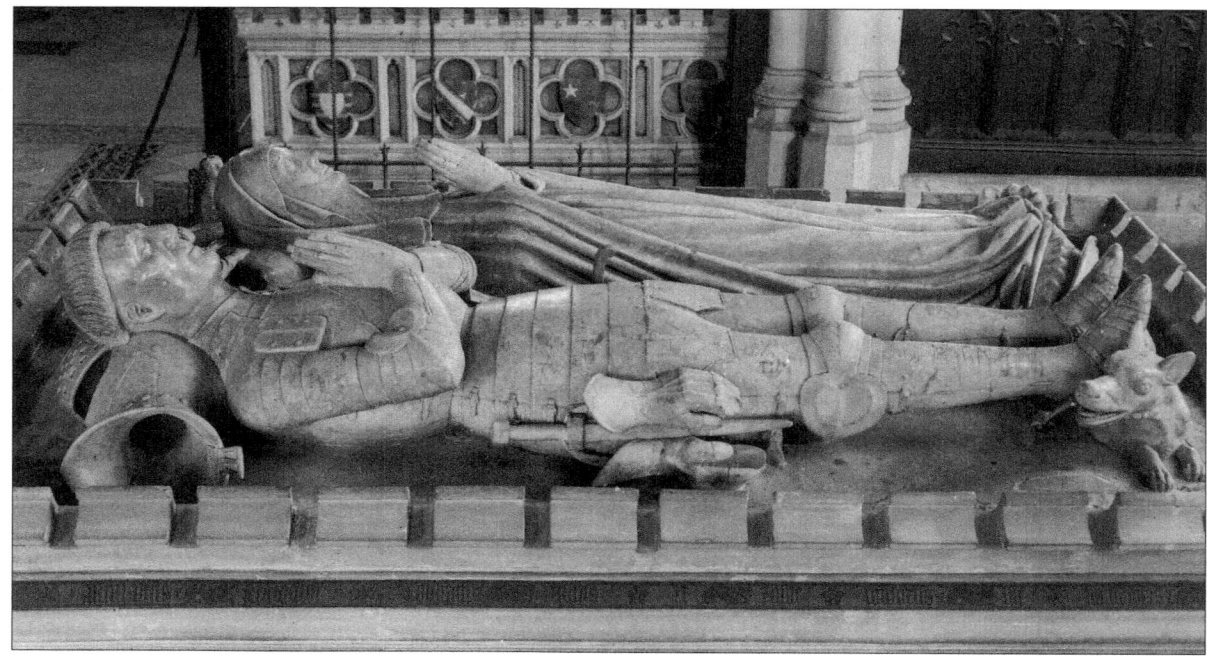

ABOVE **The effigy of Sir Reginald Cobham in Lingfield church, about 1446. The long fauld now has tassets, and his gauntlets are buttoned over the dagger. Note the bowl crop hair-style.**

RIGHT **Effigies of Lady Margaret Holland and her two husbands, Thomas, Duke of Clarence (left, died 1421), and Sir John Beaufort, Earl of Somerset (died 1410), in Canterbury Cathedral. Both knights wear tabards over their armour, and great basinets.**

A west European sallet of about 1450, from the church at Witton-le-Wear in County Durham. (By courtesy of Board of Trustees of the Armouries, AL.44 1, on loan to the Royal Armouries from the church of St Philip and St James, Witton-le-Wear)

Daggers usually had triangular-sectioned blades. The **rondel dagger** had a disc of metal or sometimes wood set at either end of the handle, or else a disc and conical pommel. **Ballock daggers** had two swellings (of wood, bone or brass) at the base of a handle of wood, bone or ivory.

The lance, often of ash, had swellings either side of the hand, and a large circular steel vamplate nailed on to guard it. A circular fixture (called a **graper**) nailed on behind the hand to ram against the lance-rest was used on the breastplate to prevent the weapon running back when a strike was made. The war-hammer sometimes had a rear spike and eventually a top spike. Maces had flanged steel heads and usually iron or steel hafts; they could be hung from the saddle by a thong. In the early years of the century the long-hafted axe was occasionally used. The **pollaxe** ('poll' meaning head) or ravensbill had a combination of axehead, hammer or beak; the top and bottom of the haft were fitted with a spike. A **rondel** protected the hand, while long steel or **latten** strips (langets) were nailed to the haft below the head to prevent it being cut. The **halberd** had a long blade backed by a fluke, with langets and top spike. The less common **ahlespiess** had a four-sided spike with a disc at the base. Bills, glaives and **guisarmes** were more common in the hands of ordinary footsoldiers.

Horses

A knight needed horses, without them he was not a knight, even though many fought on foot more than on horseback. The most prized possession was the warhorse, which might be one of two types. The largest and heaviest horse was the **destrier**, a word derived from the French for 'right' and which probably meant that it was led on the right side by a varlet. It has also been suggested that such horses were trained to lead with the right leg. Destriers were extremely valuable; some, indeed, were used only in tournaments. Their cost indicates that they were specially bred for stamina, with deep bodies for good lungs, and thick, powerful necks. However, they were not slow and could turn nimbly enough; nor were they the size of a carthorse, as is popularly imagined. Surviving 15th-century armour would never fit a carthorse, and shows that such animals were about the size of a heavy hunter. They were always stallions, and there is some evidence that their natural aggression was utilised by training them to bite and kick opponents.

In battle many rode a **courser**, an expensive warhorse but of slightly poorer quality than a destrier. In addition a good **palfrey** with a comfortable gait was required as a travelling mount. A knight might afford several riding and warhorses. As well as these there were serviceable horses for his varlets, probably **rouncys** or 'ronsons'. The **hackney**, or 'hack', was a cheaper mount for other servants or soldiers. The knight also had to provide pack animals, either sumpters, mules or draught animals for supply wagons.

19

ORGANISATION

By the 15th century feudalism had given way to a new form of raising troops. Instead of lords granting fiefs (parcels of land) in return for supplying troops, they now contracted men to fight for them. This has been called 'bastard feudalism'. A captain would agree to provide the king with a set number of men and the agreement was written twice on a contract, which was perforated and cut into two parts, one copy for the Exchequer and one for the captain. The cut was deliberately wavy or zig-zag, so that the two halves could be matched exactly if there was any dispute over the arrangements. The irregular line gave such a document its name: an indenture.

At the time of English expeditions to France, the Exchequer usually released half the agreed cash, and the rest on embarkation, following a muster to check the actual numbers had been found. Contracts contained such details as troop numbers and type (usually men-at-arms, called 'lances', and archers); they set out the muster points and times, pay, discipline, plunder (usually a third), and length of service. The latter varied from a few months to two years, though six months was common. Much of the information became standardised but was amended to suit the campaign. Sometimes the king made a single great indenture to a noble who would in any case then sub-indent other captains to make up the numbers.

Not all the soldiers knew the captains they came to fight for. In a similar way, a captain contracted troops for a fixed wage over a fixed period, a retainer's contract being validated by the lord's wax seal instead of that of the king. The second copy was retained by the man, who was known as a retainer. In March 1402 John Norbury covenanted to retain in his pay Bonifacius de Provana and a retinue of 60 lances and 60 crossbowmen for one year. Indentures also included obligations to the lord, not all of them military. Often indentures to a nobleman were made for life.

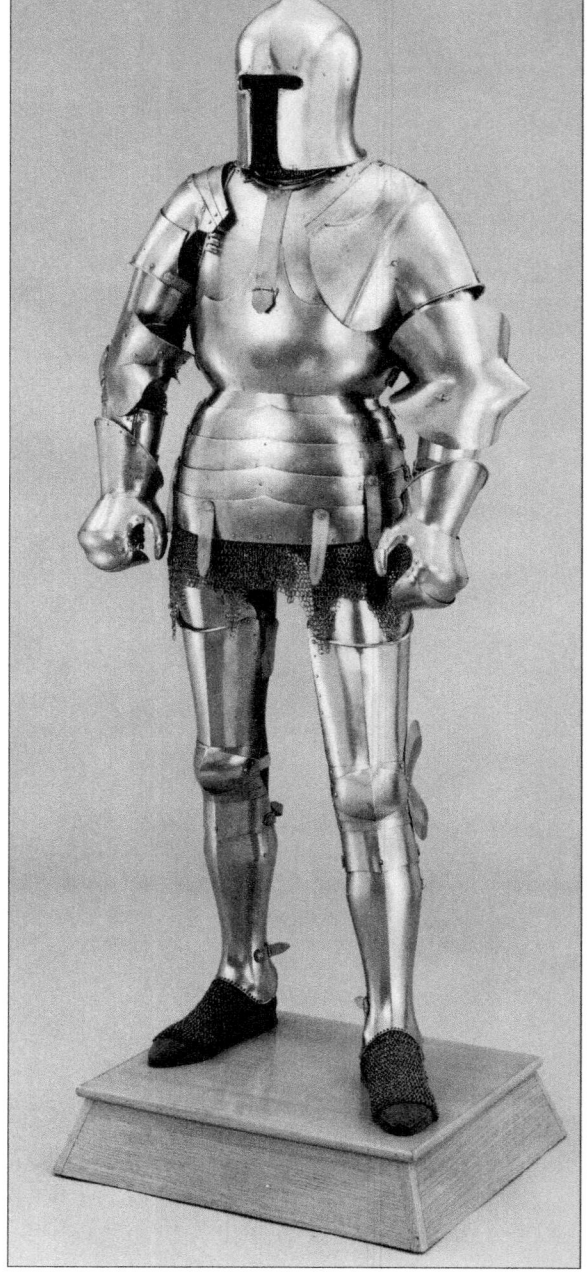

The governing of indentured companies was covered during the Hundred Years War by the issuing of ordinances of war. These were instructions to ensure such bodies of troops were properly controlled, that men did not leave or come to the army unless so ordered, and to make sure that captains themselves did not employ underhand means to fill their ranks by luring men from other companies.

The expeditionary armies in Henry VI's reign rarely exceeded about 2,000 men, except for aggressive campaigns or when the English presence was threatened. The agreed contract did not always bring in the correct

ratio of troops, and sometimes larger numbers of archers were employed and fewer men-at-arms, archers presumably being easier to recruit than mounted men-at-arms, and cheaper – 6d a day as against 12d. It is possible also that the long periods expected in overseas service did not appeal to a number of English knights as much as to professional soldiers.

By the 15th century only about five to ten per cent of men-at-arms in English armies were knights, the rest being esquires and 'gentlemen'. By mid-century some men-at-arms were not even of this rank. At the beginning of the century the ratio of archers to every man-at-arms had risen to 3:1, so that, on average, each man-at-arms was served by a page or varlet plus three archers, the latter usually mounted for mobility, though they fought on foot. This composition was essentially the same as the European 'lance', though this unit appellation and form of recruitment was not customary in England during the Wars of the Roses. Contingents could vary wildly, from a mere handful of men to a sizeable force. The selection from the retinue of Henry V in 1415 in British Library MS Sloane 6400 gives some indication:

John Irby, Esq – single man-at-arms and two foot archers
Sir John Greseley – two men-at-arms and six foot archers
Sir Thomas Tunstall – six men-at-arms and 18 mounted archers
Thomas, Earl of Salisbury – 40 men-at-arms (three knights, 36 esquires) and 80 mounted archers
Thomas, Earl of Dorset – 100 men-at-arms (one banneret, six knights, 92 esquires) and 300 mounted archers
Humphrey, Duke of Gloucester – 200 men-at-arms (six knights, 193 esquires) and 600 mounted archers

The variation in army size can be seen from the fact that, in 1415, Henry V fielded perhaps 900 men-at-arms and 5,000 archers, whereas at Verneuil in 1424 there were about 1,800 men-at-arms and between 8,000 and 9,000 archers.

Normandy

By the 15th century, a shift in strategy meant that the mobile expeditionary forces in France were being replaced in Normandy by more expensive garrisons. Annual indentures were drawn up between the king, or his regent, and garrison captains, followed by quarterly commissions of array for musters. Pay was given each quarter after approval of the muster rolls. Initially men from the conquering army made up garrisons, later supplemented by volunteers from England or from troops still in France, some of whom settled there. It has been estimated that in 1420 there were 1,028 men-at-arms and 2,926 archers in various garrisons in Normandy. Such forces ranged in size from the two men-at-arms and six archers at Pont d'Ouve to 60 men-at-arms and 180 archers at Rouen. Outside Normandy a similar situation existed, though Calais and its march had 1,120 men under Henry V.

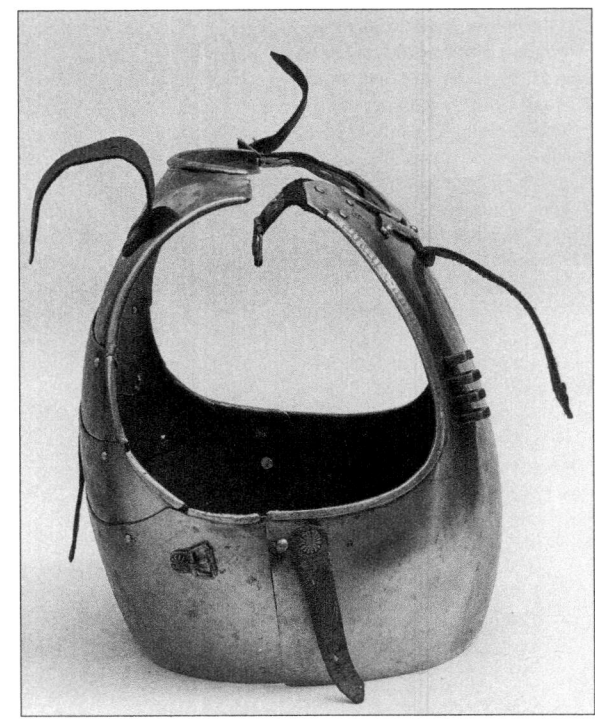

In 1433 the English government claimed to have 7,000–8,000 men in France; this would not have included the garrison of Guyenne and feudal troops from Normandy. John, Duke of Bedford, regent for the young Henry VI, had 100 household men and 300 archers. Some Frenchmen also served Henry V after lands north of the Loire were ceded to him in 1420, while Norman forces often fought alongside Englishmen. Between 1422 and 1450 about 45 castles and towns were regularly garrisoned. A ratio of three archers to one man-at-arms was usual, with more footsoldiers in coastal areas. Garrisons increased and decreased in line with the French threat.

For field service in Normandy, swift mobilisation was needed; requirements such as escorting supply trains or siege work could last from a few days to several months, and involve a few hundred or several thousand men. Some men were recruited from retinues such as Bedford's (less after about 1430) or from the many ex-soldiers living on the land some were drawn from garrisons, and some from those given land in return for a feudal obligation to serve.

Livery and maintenance

Great lords employed knights and men-at-arms in private retinues, indeed sometimes so many that they formed private armies. Under this system of 'livery and maintenance', the retainers wore their lord's coat with his livery colours, usually the two principal colours from his coat of arms, and they were maintained at his expense. It was a practice that meant nobles could field large bodies of troops and were a permanent threat to stability. Violence on occasions spilled out into open warfare

with heavy casualties, and it was the duty of the king or noble to intervene to stop quarrels getting out of hand. A strong king was necessary in such circumstances and a weak or unlucky monarch could find himself on the end of a revolt.

It was the king's lot to pass titles and land rights to his nobles, and for them to pass them through their own heirs and retainers as best they could. However, the nobles and gentry had the wherewithal in men and money to resort to violence if necessary when involved in disputes. These were sometimes valid questions of land ownership or rights, but could also concern cases of simple avarice:

'... the squire is not satisfied unless he lives like a knight; the knight wants to be a baron; the baron an earl; the earl a king.'

If they could not be controlled by the upper strata of society through the crown's active intervention, then unrest would break out as private quarrels were pursued by force of arms. Always a threat, this problem increased during the Wars of the Roses, when families joined opposite sides in order to carry on private vendettas.

Retainers could be called out at any time, and acted as bodyguards for their lord, accompanying him around the countryside, to his manors, to the court or tournament, or to war. They learned their trade as squires, yeomen or grooms, and wore their lord's livery. The *Black Book of Edward IV* gives the following guide to the maximum number of retainers allowed by various ranks of noblemen:

King: 600	Viscount: 80
Duke: 240	Baron: 40
Marquis: 200	Knight: 16
Earl: 140	

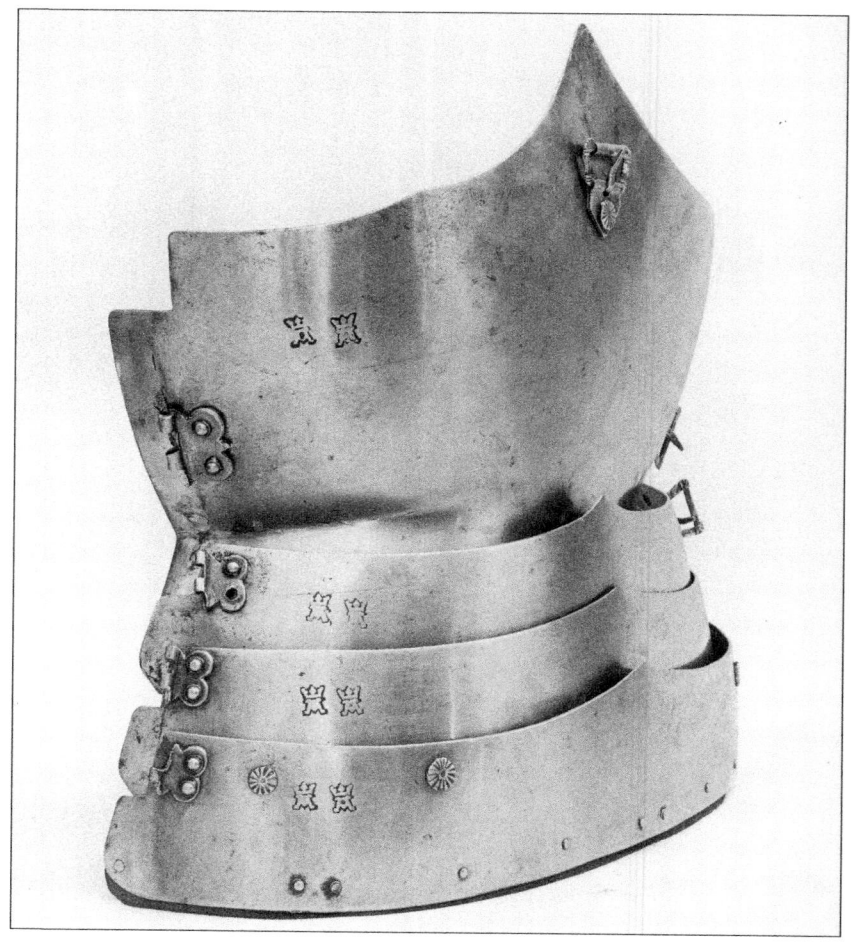

For the duration of the Wars of the Roses, some 35 years, a maximum of about 50,000 men were ever in arms at one time, usually in short campaigns.

It was, however, difficult to maintain a force of ideal size, especially with an itinerant aristocracy, when for example a retainer might arrive at his lord's house or castle with his own followers.

Some lived so far away that they were known as 'extraordinary retainers'. As with the old feudal practice of being enfeoffed to more than one lord, so retainers might hold contracts of several masters, which gave them more money, more chance of receiving favours and better protection. These men were known as 'well willers'. The problems caused by the common practice of being retained to more than one lord meant that a retainer was careful to insert clauses in his contract which excused him from having to face one of his other employers on the battlefield.

By contrast, those closest to their lord had no contract but lived by the older bond of loyalty. This practice means that there might have been many more men retained than is evident from records. The bond between retainers and their lord could be strong, a trait that compared to an aristocrat's bond with his king, such as the example of William, Lord Hastings, and Edward IV. When speed of action was necessary it

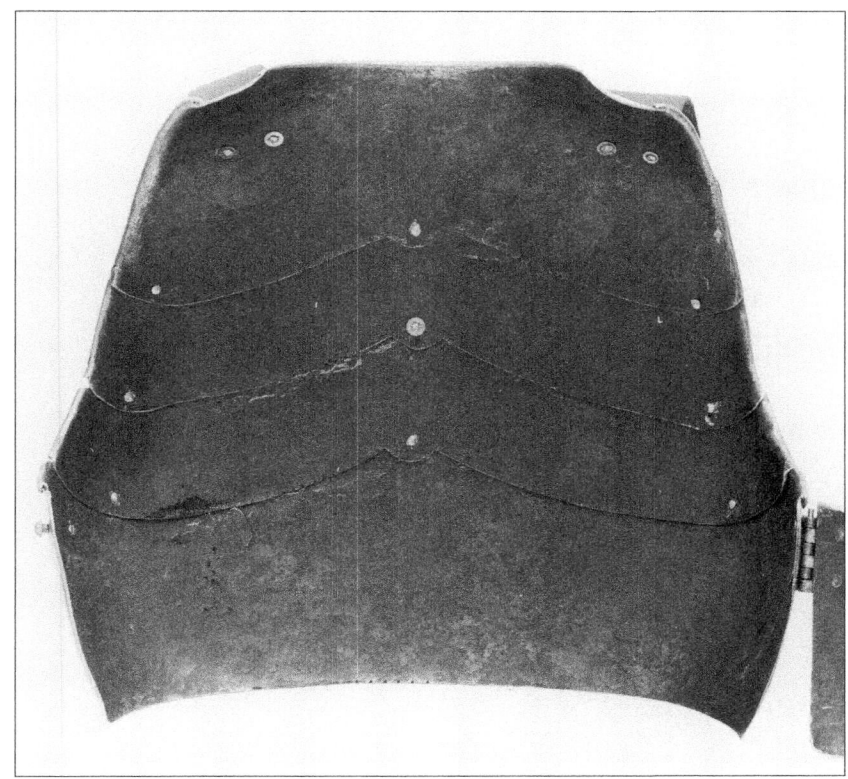

was the household retainers or 'feed men', who were close at hand, that were called upon. The same men were also convenient to form a guard and escort for their lord on visits to estates or other lords or the king's court. At times of war, however, enough men had to remain to look after a lord's estates and to see that crop production was carried on as usual.

A knightly retainer would have to supply a number of men to his lord, who often had many retainers. An indenture dated 20 September 1468 between Anthony, Lord Scales, and John Norbury Esquire was for one man-at-arms and 118 archers for 91 days. Indentures like this enabled the lord to supply the king with an agreed number of men while still keeping plenty for his own use. The most powerful nobles could call upon many thousands of men. In 1484 the Duke of Norfolk could raise 1,000 retainers and levies from his East Anglian estates alone.

Archers would usually make up the largest proportion of the men a retainer could call up from his own estates. Billmen or soldiers carrying other staff weapons usually made up the remainder. Men-at-arms, who might fight mounted or on foot, were more likely to come from a retainer's own family or men in his household, again a small number compared to the archers. Unlike in the early part of the century, the ratio of archers to men-at-arms had changed noticeably, and could be as high as 8:1. For Edward IV's expedition to France a knight was paid two shillings a day, an esquire one shilling.

During the Wars of the Roses there was a revival in the use of 'Commissions of Array', the summoning of town and county militias, particularly by the Lancastrians. Such men had to be 'well and defencibly arrayed' according to the proclamation of 1463, which demanded that every man between the ages of 16 and 60 in 16 counties be ready to serve Edward IV at a day's notice. The ordering and enforcement of the Commissions usually fell to the sheriff of each county concerned. Nobles too might summon militias. In 1471 the Earl of Warwick decreed death for anyone shirking his call to the militia, and the demands increasingly became less choosy about exactly who was called up. Large numbers of militia were, according to a commission of 1468, divided into companies of 1,000 men, subdivided into groups of 20 and 100. However, because of the fickle nature of loyalties, and the bitterness inherent in civil wars, troops might join whichever faction they preferred, regardless of the original summons. On occasion both sides called up the same militia force.

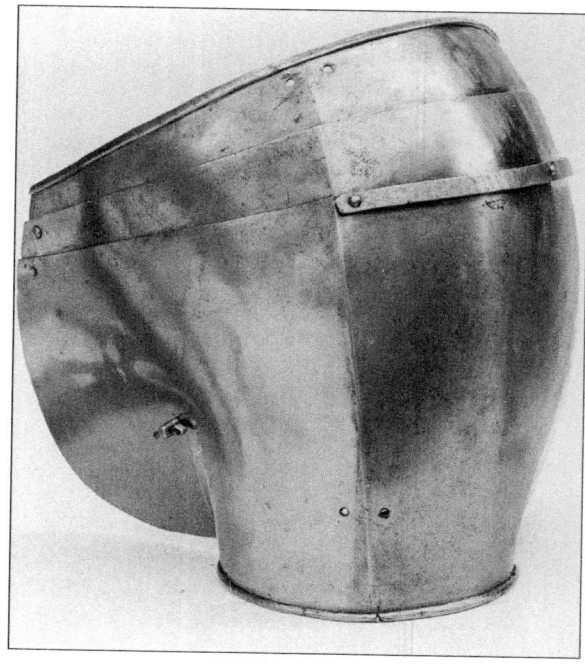

An inventory of Sir John Fastolf's possessions taken in 1448 mentions silk surcoats embroidered with his armourial bearings. Another in 1461 reveals that his castle at Caister was well defended by four breech-loading guns with eight chambers, two firing 7 in (15 cm) stone balls, two firing 5 in (12 cm) stones. A serpentine with three chambers fired a 10 in (25 cm) stone, another a 7 in (15 cm) stone. Three fowlers fired 12 in (30 cm) stones, whilst he also had two short guns for ships (he owned several for trade) with six chambers. Two small serpentines and four guns lying in stocks fired lead pellets. There were also seven handguns and equipment for the guns. Together with this firepower were 24 shields of elm, two of whalebone; eight old-fashioned suits of white armour; ten pairs of body armour, worn out; 14 horn jackets, worn out; ten basinets; 24 sallets; six gorgets; 16 lead hammers; nine bills; other pieces of armour and weapons; zinc caps; wire of little value; four great crossbows of steel; two of whalebone; four of yew; two habergeons and a barrel to store them in.

CAMPAIGN LIFE

Life for the knight on campaign could be miserable or comfortable, depending on several factors. The actual rank of a knight would play a large part. A duke took several tents, campaign furniture, even hangings for the interior of his tent, and copious supplies of food and wine. A poor knight took what he could afford: a tent for himself, and supplies for his few followers.

The setting for the campaign also affected the way a knight lived. English armies in France could, when necessary, take food from the surrounding countryside or from captured towns, in which case a knight with a keen eye could see himself and his men well stocked. The *chevauchée* was also a good way to deny the enemy his own provisions, and it was a slap in the face to the lord supposedly protecting the area. Similarly, booty was forthcoming, either from battlefield plunder, items from towns or else from ransoming important prisoners, who were far more willing to give themselves up to another knight than to a ruffian archer or billman. The benefits of plunder, however, might be offset by the knowledge that the army could be on campaign for weeks or months, that sieges were liable to drag on, and that, especially in the latter case, disease was very likely to strike. The campaigning season for medieval armies was traditionally the months from spring until autumn, but in reality knights found themselves on campaign in less than ideal conditions. The battle at Towton in Yorkshire, fought in a bitter blizzard in March 1461, is well known, the battle of Wakefield fought the December before is less so.

It was a captain's duty to ensure that his men were kept under control where possible. Henry V forbade plundering in France and hanged an archer who stole a pyx from a church. However, Henry did endeavour to ensure that his men were paid and adequately fed, though even he could not always prevent the slaughter and looting that followed the fall of a town, as happened at Caen in 1417. Since this was accepted practice in cases where surrender had initially been refused, there was little even the king could do.

When a town was taken, a garrison was installed, including knights, all commanded by a captain. Some knights might remain in the town for years, or at least until their contract expired. If single they might even marry French womenfolk. During Henry V's reign some knights would have settled in Normandy, being granted estates in return for military duties. Nobles would also have received large parcels of land in return for duties such as the upkeep of the local castle and its garrison.

Much of a campaign was taken up in marching, in hot sun and soaking rain, over unmade roads sometimes turned to bogs. Often knights sat in front of a castle for weeks with little to do unless an assault

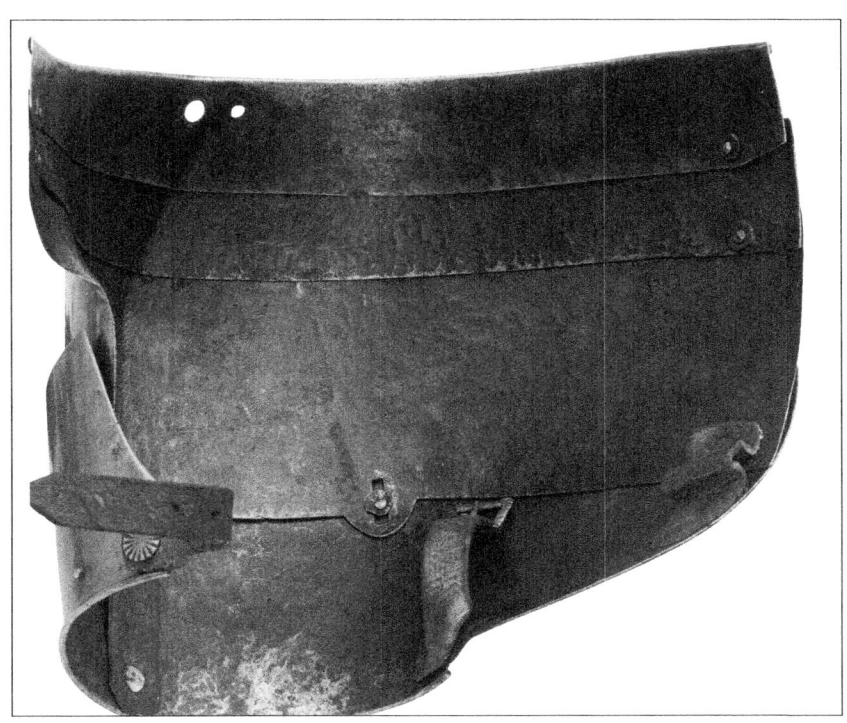

An Italian horse armour made by Pier Innocenzo da Faerno in about 1450. This is the earliest almost complete equestrian armour to survive, though the flanchards for the flanks are missing. (Historisches Museum der Stadt Wien)

was planned, but the chance to win renown via a scaling ladder was also highly dangerous. Sometimes knights would ride off with their escorts to visit a tournament, where rules of chivalry would prevent them being arrested.

A typical knight had several followers, at least one of whom would have been a varlet, whose duty it was to look after his master. Damaged armour would need repairing by the armourers who moved with the army; swords had to be honed. The knight's followers would find him lodgings or tents that could be paid for with coin, or else would erect his own tent.

A knight's status meant that he also had money enough to pay for food or other items. However, a noble had to rely on his retainers, his household and feed men, to supply the hardcore of his forces. These were the only reliable followers he had, some of them were knights like himself, who went with him in peace or war. The retainers themselves also brought tenants, but if these tenants refused to come, or deserted, if the arrayed troops supplied to the lord did not materialise, then he could not deliver an effective force for a campaign. Mercenaries included Welsh lords who, like their English equivalent, tended to join whichever side suited their own ideas for striking at old enemies.

In England during the Wars of the Roses, the campaigns tended to be much shorter. For one thing England is much smaller than France, but there were significantly few sieges of towns or cities during this period, most of the conflict taking the form of violent battles or skirmishes. Despite this, Andrew Boardman, using figures by A. Goodman, has calculated that an average campaign lasted only 23 days. However, it was not foreign soil over which the armies marched, and therefore any pillaging would cause widespread distrust and unrest amongst the king's subjects; the only exception was campaigns into Scotland during this period.

Commanders were aware that if money ran short then pay and food supply suffered and men would desert. It meant that the troops were best recruited and moved swiftly while they were relatively happy. The author of the *Boke of Noblesse*, which was addressed to Edward IV before his French expedition in 1475, suggests that unpleasant excesses by troops in earlier campaigns were caused by a lack of proper and regular pay. One factor made these campaigns different from those in the earlier part of the century. Lords and arrayed troops often chose the opposite side to that of a rival so they could resolve differences by force. Thus a number of titled men perished, being killed on the field or executed afterwards instead of being taken prisoner for ransom, such was the sense of revenge felt by families for one another. The chivalric code between knights was passed over in the pursuit of bloody retribution, and the chance of dying a violent death during a campaign was perhaps greater than had previously been the case.

The necessities of war

In order to carry enough provisions for a large force, many wagons were needed, sometimes more than could reasonably be procured. The armour of the captains, armoured knights and other retainers would be carried in carts, the pieces perhaps wrapped in hay in locked barrels, but other soldiers, both mounted and foot, carried their own, together with any spares, a blanket and a day's food ration. Food was an obvious essential, together with ale and wine casks. However, room also had to be made for the large number of arrow sheaves carried for the use of the archers, each bound sheaf consisting of about 24 shafts. Spare heads and shafts were also necessary.

A well-armed force might also have cannon in its train, for which specially cut stone balls or, towards the end of the century, cast iron balls, had to be carried, as well as gunpowder and all the paraphernalia necessary to lay and fire the guns: rammers, powder ladles, sponges, scourers, linstocks, etc. Occasionally older forms of siege engines, such as catapults (some built on site or from transported sections) and sheds were called upon, requiring ropes, grease and nails. Mobile forges were a necessity both for armourers and farriers. Bedding and tents for the wealthier men, together with creature comforts – folding chairs, beds, sideboards, chests of various sizes – added to the bulk of material carried. As well as food for the troops, fodder was sometimes also carried for the horses used by mounted contingents, and for pack animals and draught horses or oxen.

The Coventry sallet of about 1460 may be one of the few surviving English-made pieces of armour. The high skull is different from the forms seen in Italy and especially Germany. (Herbert Art Gallery and Museum, Coventry)

Despite all these preparations, food and drink sometimes ran short, especially where a large force was concerned, and had to be either taken by force or bought in bulk from towns or cities. For this, large amounts of money had to be carried in barrels or chests. Scourers, victuallers or harbingers rode ahead of the army to locate towns on the route of march and agree sales of provisions, as well as billets if necessary. However, supply carts, pulled by teams of horses or oxen, were rather vulnerable targets. The Duke of York found this out when one such train, returning laden with vital provisions purchased by his scourers from Wakefield in 1460, and needed for a force of only 5,000 men, was pounced on by Lancastrians near Sandal Castle. His attempt to rescue it ended in his defeat and death at the battle of Wakefield.

As earlier in the century, some knights formed part of a castle garrison. These were retainers of great lords given control of fortifications, the most powerful being the marcher lords in the north, the families of Neville (warden of the West March) and Percy (warden of the East March). These men, who had control of the northern borders, could field powerful forces if necessary, and it was fortunate for the king during the first part of the conflict that the two families felt enough rivalry to prevent them from forming a dangerous northern coalition. The king's deliberate support for one family over the other

A grisaille of about 1460 by Guillaume Vreland shows an armourer cold hammering a plate while another burnishes a breastplate. (Friedrich-Alexander-Universität Erlangen-Nürnberg)

helped keep them divided. The castles themselves only seem to have held small garrisons, of perhaps 20 or so men. A far larger garrison was posted in Calais, over 1,000 men to protect the march and the fortifications of Hammes and Guinnes, together with the English wool staple. Political unrest adversely affected cash flow, and this caused dangerous tension in the garrison, as in 1460 when the soldiers broke into the wool warehouses to take the payment due to them.

INTO BATTLE

The knight of the 15th century often fought on foot. He had been trained to fight mounted, with a lance, but it was often more effective to dismount most of the men-at-arms and to keep only a small mounted reserve. This was partly due to the increasing threat from missiles. In France during the early 15th century, the English forces used tactics learned the previous century. If the armoured fighting men were kept near the blocks of archers and all waited for the enemy to advance, it meant the latter arrived in a more tired state, all the while harassed by the arrows from the archers and compressed by a natural tendency to shy away from them. This bunching could then work to the advantage of the English who used their archers to strike at the press of French soldiers, now aggravated by those behind pushing forward, as happened at Agincourt. The groups of mounted men-at-arms who tried to outflank the archers at the start of the battle were foiled by the woods which protected each end of the English line, and found to their cost the price of facing archers when mounted.

When archers were in a strong position, ideally defended by stakes, hedges or ditches, a cavalry charge was extremely dangerous. But even when the horses were protected by armour, there was always some exposed part that an arrow could strike, and arrows went deep. Shafts fitted with broad hunting heads made short work of flesh, and the horses became unmanageable even when not mortally wounded. The mounted knight then became useless as he fought for control or was thrown to the ground as the animal collapsed. It is worth noting that only a few hundred at each end of the French line attacked, and of these a few still reached the stakes despite the volleys of presumably thousands of arrows launched at them. Yet it was the dismounted men-at-arms who did most of the fighting in this battle, and it was they who, according to one chronicler, pushed the English line back a spear's length before everything became jammed up:

'But when the French nobility, who at first approached in full front, had nearly joined battle, either from fear of the arrows, which by their impetuosity pierced through the sides and bevors of their basinets, or that they might more speedily penetrate our ranks to the banners, they divided themselves into three troops, charging our line in three places

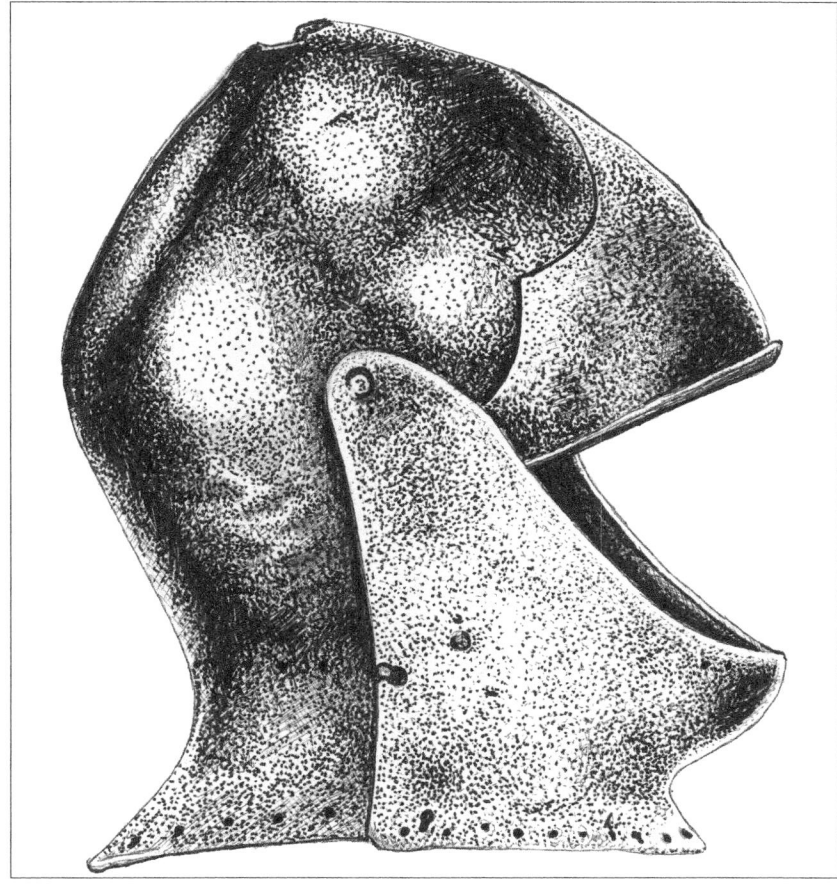

A sallet/close helmet of about 1485, from Pluckley Church, Kent and now in the Royal Armouries. This very rare form of helmet is known from two other English examples and the Beauchamp Pageant, all with English connections. It may be English, Italian or Flemish made for the English market, and has a pivoting bevor. It originally had a riveted reinforcing bevor covering the lower edge of the missing visor. The apex has been pierced to fit a funerary crest spike.

where the banners were: and intermingling their spears closely, they assaulted our men with so ferocious an impetuosity, that they compelled them to retreat almost at spear's length'.

Arrows versus armour

Archers carried specialist arrows, with needle-pointed heads called bodkins, to cut through armour. Tests have shown that the spin of the arrow in flight enables short bodkins striking at right angles to drill a hole into armour plate, but that the slight shoulders at the back of the arrow head then force it out again. However, long bodkins, were slimmer and could penetrate plate enough to do damage. The range at which an arrow was shot, as well as whether iron or steel heads were used, would determine its potency. At short range, the bodkins could be lethal, or inflict a wound that would slow up or debilitate a man in armour. However, most surviving oxidised red bodkins seem to be of iron, which tests suggest curl up when they strike plate. If they struck mail they would burst the rings apart as they went through. Crossbows were equally powerful although they did not employ bodkins. Handguns were also now appearing in armies, though not in any great number at this period.

Since plate armour obviated the need for a shield, and fighting dismounted meant the rein hand was free, it became common for knights on foot to carry a two-handed staff weapon in addition to the sword hanging at their side. At first this was often a lance cut down to a length of around 6–7 ft (1.8–2.1 m). Increasingly, other staff weapons were carried, which could deal more effectively with plate armour. One of the most popular was the pollaxe, designed to dent or crush the plates, either to wound the wearer or so damage the plates that they ceased to function properly.

Mounted men were very useful in a rout, for they could catch up a fleeing enemy and cut him down with minimum risk to themselves, especially if he was lightly armoured. Indeed, catching archers out of position was the best way for cavalry to scatter them before they got a chance to deploy. In the Hundred Years War this was not too much of a problem for English knights, since the French did not use archers on a large scale. During the Wars of the Roses, archers fought on both sides in Yorkist and Lancastrian armies and, for the most part, the

A late 15th-century depiction of the Duke of Orleans, captured at Agincourt in 1415, as a prisoner in the Tower of London, one of several castles in which he was incarcerated while awaiting ransom. He seems to be represented several times: arriving by river, signing his release papers in the White Tower (the large donjon), watching at a window for the messenger, embracing him and then riding out. (By permission of the British Library, MS Royal 16F II, ff.72v-73)

B: Knight, c.1425

B

C: Confrontation on the road, 22 May 1448

C

D: At the Kingmaker's court, 1465

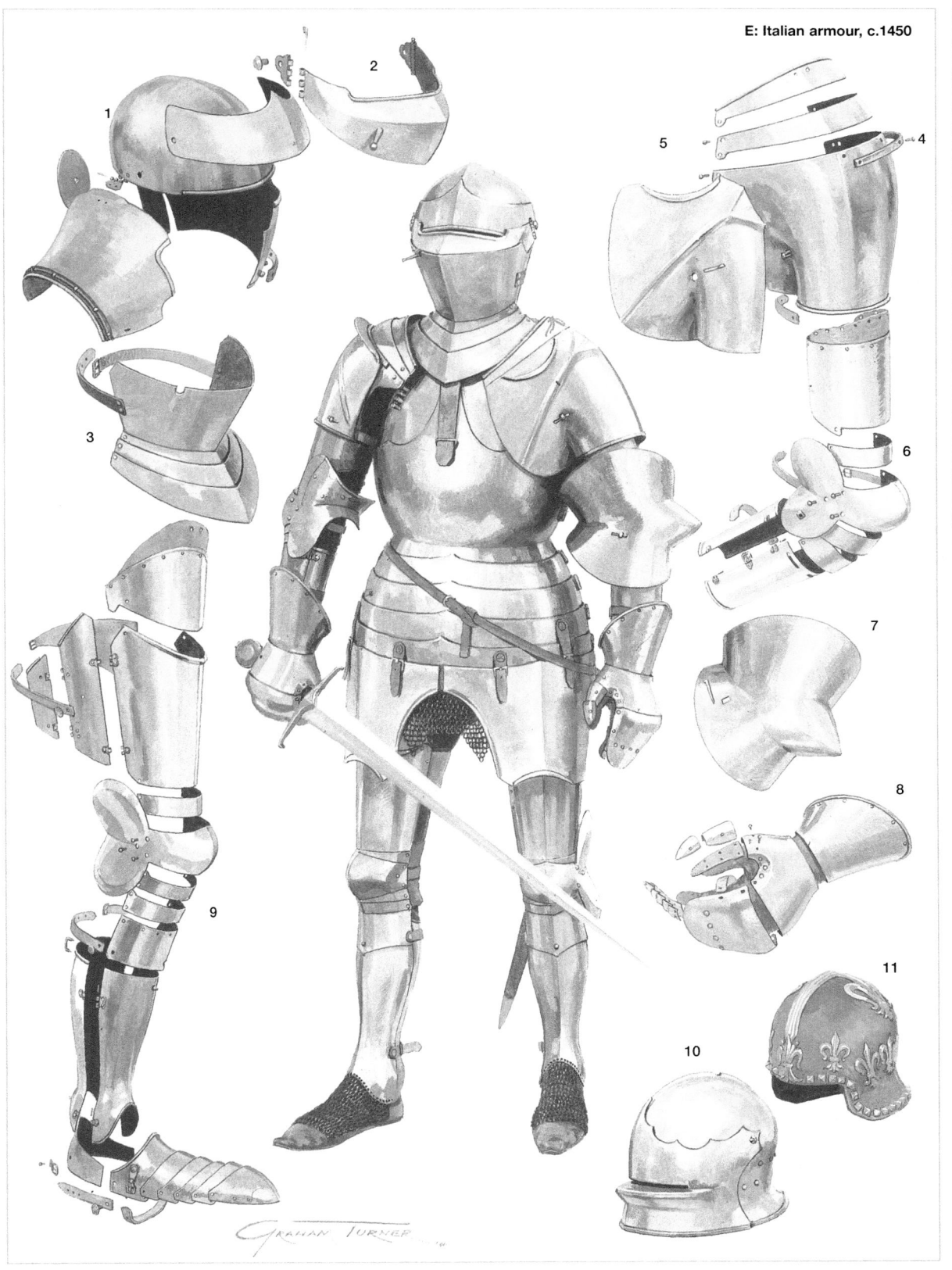

1

2

5

4

3

6

7

8

9

11

10

GRAHAM TURNER

F: English armour, 1450–1500

G: Equipment, second half of the 15th century

G

H: Tournament armour

H

I: The battle of Wakefield, 31 December 1460

J: The consequences of defeat

men-at-arms found it best to stick with the tried-and-trusted methods and fight on foot.

Organisation and identification

Armies still tended to organise themselves into three divisions or 'battles', as they had in previous centuries: the vanguard or 'van', the main battle and the rearguard. Each division included soldiers of all types who served the various lords or the king. A man of rank, be he **banneret**, lord or king, was recognised by his banner, a large square or rectangular flag bearing his coat-of-arms. The lord might also wear a surcoat with his arms, at first a tight or loose **jupon** with or without sleeves, latterly a loose tabard with loose elbow-length sleeves rather like that worn by **heralds**. However, surcoats were increasingly discarded and, with a lack of shields, it was essential that the banner-bearer remain close to his master, following his horse's tail, as it was said. The rallying flag was the standard, a long flag ending in a point or swallow tail. It was usually divided horizontally into the two principal colours from the lord's coat-of-arms, which also formed the livery colours worn on the jackets of his retainers. The end nearest the fly was usually furnished with a red cross of St George on a white ground. Along the rest of the flag were symbols from the coat-of-arms, together with heraldic badges, again repeated in the badges sewn on to livery jackets or worn in hats. A lord might give the order not to move more than ten feet (or a similar measurement) from the standards, but if the line slightly shifted it would not be too difficult in the confusion of battle to strike out accidentally at an ally.

Knights fighting mounted might have their coat-of-arms on a small pointed pennon nailed to their lance. In order to carry out heraldic

Oxburgh Hall, Suffolk, was built in brick in about 1480. The home of the Bedingfield family, it blends the idea of a castle with the fortified manor. The large windows and false machicolations on the gatehouse turrets show that this is not a serious military building.

identification and to deliver messages, important nobles employed their own heralds wearing tabards of their master's arms, and trumpeters with the arms on hangings below the instruments.

The noise of many men hammering away at each other must have been deafening. When the visor was down, it was not only the hearing but also the vision that was impaired, though lateral views were better than might be supposed. Helmets lacking ventilation holes made it difficult for the wearer to see his own feet without bending forward, and they also quickly became hot and sweaty.

CHIVALRY

The strange force that bound together knights from all over Europe was chivalry, a word whose French roots show its original association with horses and horsemanship. By the 15th century it had come to include the essential qualities expected of a knight: good manners, respect for women, protection of the church and the poor, courage in the face of the enemy. All these ideals had become increasingly fused together during the centuries and were to be heard in the romances which were told and retold in knightly halls and courts throughout Europe. Knighthood too was a bond, since knights shared a common interest and were of a certain rank in society. Knights recognised foreign names and faces from tournaments in which they had fought opposite one another (or sometimes together), or from court visits. Such intercourse often bred respect for a worthy opponent.

However, chivalry was also in some respects a game, a courtly pursuit where gentlemen could show off their breeding and knowledge of how to behave in polite society, especially in the presence of ladies. They knew full well that in war chivalry often went by the board.

Richard Beauchamp is knighted by Henry VI, an early 15th-century scene shown in the costume worn later that century. (By permission of the British Library, MS Cotton Julius E IV, art. 6, f.2v)

Knights might well spare one another out of respect or humanity, but often more from a sense of lucrative gain to be made from a fat ransom. This was seen especially in France during the first part of the century. Indeed, such profits could be ploughed back into land and castles, such as Ampthill in Bedfordshire, built from spoils taken by Lord Fanhope in France. In 1421 two English esquires, John Winter and Nicholas Molyneux, agreed to become brothers in arms in the wars in France, to pool their winnings and use them in England to buy lands and manors. However, a tight situation called for drastic measures. The massacre of knightly prisoners at Agincourt by order of King Henry V himself is a case in point – Henry ignoring chivalry at a moment in the battle where the captured Frenchmen might take up arms as soon as the English were preoccupied with fresh attacks that now threatened them.

Increasingly, bands of professional men-at-arms were seen on the battlefields of Europe, men to whom a coat-of-arms was a relatively unimportant symbol that carried with it expectations of courage in the face of extreme danger which many of them preferred not to stay and

The Dauphin defeated by Sir Richard Beauchamp, who wears an armet with plume and heraldic tabard over his armour. Others wear open or visored sallets, with kettle hats also seen on the right of the picture. Some wear brigandines. English longbowmen oppose French crossbowmen. (By permission of the British Library, MS Cotton Julius E IV, art. 6, f.20v)

face. Such moral courage was not profitable and the absence of recognisable arms prevented a slur on the family name. In England the practice of sparing men of rank was increasingly marred during the Wars of the Roses. Now families joined opposing sides in the hope of being able to use this opportunity to settle old grievances. Such motives did not sit well with chivalrous ideals, and those on the losing side might well find themselves at the receiving end of the *coup de grace* instead of a proffered hand.

Chivalry was also used in diplomacy. Occasionally an effort was made to prevent a war by the offer of single combat between champions. Though frequently no more than verbiage, in 1425 Philip the Good of France made a serious challenge to Duke Humphrey of Gloucester, and even went into training and took fencing lessons. Despite having arms and tents made ready for the expected combat, diplomacy won the day and the contest never took place.

The great English secular order of chivalry was that of the Garter, established by Edward III in 1348. Most of the Knights of the Garter were military officials of the English crown, and this military background was a necessary part of the qualification for entry for those

The battle of Agincourt, as imagined in the later 15th century. Note how the horses only wear shaffrons and, in one case, a crinet. The swords are acutely pointed (Lambeth Palace Library, MS 6, f.233)

not of royal birth, until Thomas Cromwell became the first 'secular' member in the 16th century.

A knight could be degraded and removed from the order of knighthood for three felonies: treason, fleeing during a battle, and heresy. Latterly wasteful living was added. The ceremony to remove a shamed man from the ranks of knighthood is illustrated in the case of Sir Ralph Grey in 1464, who was convicted of treason. His spurs were hacked off, his coat of arms torn from his body and his armour was broken up. His

sentence also decreed that his coat-of-arms be replaced by another that bore his arms reversed, but Edward IV excused him this part of the punishment.

The 15th century saw a resurgence of romance literature, resulting from a borrowing of such material in the pageants of this period. The stories of Charlemagne were translated from a 13th-century version in 1454 by Lord Berners, called *The Boke of Duke Huon of Bordeux*. New versions of stories about King Arthur were now being produced, the most famous being *Le Morte d'Arthur* of Sir Thomas Malory, which was printed by Caxton in 1485 and widely distributed. Here was an author not producing work for the king but for his own peers, gentlemen and gentlewomen. The work of the 13th-century Majorcan writer, Raimon Llull, was translated by Caxton into English as *The Book of the Ordre of Chyvalry or Knyghthode*, carried out, we are told, at the request of 'a gentyl and noble esquyer'. Other authors such as Gilbert de la Haye were also producing versions of the literature of chivalry.

Malory wrote at a time when the ideals of knighthood were subsumed by ceremonial. Lancelot, despite his weaknesses, is Malory's ideal of chivalry, rather than Galahad, since the writer viewed chivalry largely as a secular entity. He makes Arthur into a great knightly hero, drawing on English romances. Unlike in French romances, many familiar knightly names, such as Gawain, are Arthur's commanders as well as brave knights. Malory echoes the reality of English courtly life, when great lords were also the king's commanders in war. He also portrays the demise of courtly love, the idealism of holding a lady in high repute. As Iseult herself says to Tristram, love is an obstacle and will provoke ridicule in other knights for taking her with him to Arthur's court, 'A! se how Sir Trystram huntyth and hawkyth and cowryth within a castell wyth hys lady, and forsakyth us.' Personal feelings can spell doom to knighthood, as in the tragedy of Lancelot when he finally succumbs to Guinevere. It is enough that a knight perform good deeds. Caxton comments in his preface to Malory's work:

This scene of John of Gaunt feasted by the King of Portugal gives a good idea of a rich man's life in the late 15th century. Food is placed on a table from the serving hatch on the left, while musicians play. From Jean de Wavrin's *Chroniques d'Angleterre*, made in the 1470s for Edward IV. (By permission of the British Library, MS Royal 14 E IV, f.244v)

An old hermit, once a knight, instructs a squire in the values of chivalry, from the *Book of the Ordre of Chyvalry*, an English version of Raimon Llull's treatise, made about 1473–83 for Edward IV. (By permission of the British Library, MS Royal 14 E II, f.338)

'For herein may be seen noble chyvalrye, curtosye, humanyté, frendlynesse, handynesse, love, frendshyp, cowardyse, murdre, hate, vertue, and synne, but t'exersyse and folowe vertu ...'

Tournaments

The tournament was still a good place for the exercise of arms, but by now it had become as much a spectacle as a training for war. Jousts of peace between two mounted opponents with blunted lances required specialised equipment and high saddles, so that a shattered lance was increasingly the accepted outcome rather than unhorsing. By the 1420s the **tilt** had appeared in Italy, at first a cloth barrier but soon a stout wooden one, which separated the contestants to avoid collisions (deliberate or otherwise) and to help keep horses from running wide. The tilt did not help increase skill for war.

However, some still preferred jousts of war with sharp lances (*à outrance*), the armour being largely that worn in battle, and such contests were more dangerous, sometimes resulting in fatal injuries, though killing the opponent was never an objective. In one version, 'jousts at large' or 'at random', no tilt barrier was used; once the lances were dropped, the reinforces were removed and the two contestants could continue with swords. The **tourney** or team event was similar, but involved two groups. Descended from the original form of the tournament, it still provided a spectacle. The club tourney, however, differed in that only clubs or rebated swords were used. Foot combats reflected the increasing tendency to dismount in battle, though in the sport set numbers of blows were agreed and delivered, with officials intervening if this was transgressed.

As aspiring bourgeois members of society rose to knightly rank, so those who were of such rank by birth used chivalry to identify with the king to preserve their status. Hence the threat from restive lords lessened, and monarchs were less suspicious of tournaments as an umbrella for intriguing nobles. Tournaments were now seen as a reflection of a ruler's wealth and magnanimity. However, in England the expense of these festivities was becoming prohibitive, and in the 15th century they became increasingly rare. Some events were held, such as that to celebrate the coronation of Joan of Navarre, the queen of Henry IV, in February 1402, depicted in the later 15th-century *Pageant of Richard Beauchamp*. Knights wishing to participate in or view such scenes often had to travel abroad, especially to Burgundy, where the dukes put on lavish displays to emphasise their power. In the case of the *pas de la belle pèlerine*, held near Calais by the Bastard of St Pol in 1449, heralds visited England and Scotland to proclaim the event. The *pas d'armes de l'Arbre d'Or* was based on the story of Florimont, the knight of the Golden Tree who served the Lady of the Secret Isle. It was held in the market place at Bruges in July 1468, to celebrate the marriage of Charles the Bold, Duke of Burgundy, and Margaret of York. On the sixth day Lord Scales challenged the Bastard of Burgundy, whom he had fought in a duel the previous year. Such was their comradeship, now sworn brothers-in-arms, that the Bastard declined the challenge and instead asked Adolf of Cleves to step into the role of defender. There followed some excellent jousts: Cleves shattered 17 lances against Scales' 11 but the main casualty was the Bastard himself, who was kicked above the knee by a horse while he watched, and at one point was feared to be dying. After a tourney, feasting ended the whole event, with 30 centrepiece gardens each with a golden hedge and golden tree. A whale arrived accompanied by giants, and sirens appeared from the whale to sing; the giants then fought a battle with 12 sea-knights. The Duke of Burgundy was awarded the prize for the tournament but refused and gave it instead to John Woodville, the English queen's brother.

Challenges to combats *à outrance* were not uncommon in the 15th century, though these too usually involved meeting knights from other lands. These were much less spectacular than the types of displays just described and involved a variety of sharp weapons instead of the blunted lances that predominated in the *pas*. There was more variety in the combat too, with knights fighting on foot as well as mounted, as in real war. While all tournaments were risky, these combats were more dangerous. Despite this rougher quality, they too gradually acquired a courtly element, and challenges were sent out as formal letters. The knights who took part were those who enjoyed the extra thrill of fighting with sharp weapons; they might be men out to win renown, or bands of knights grouped into a kind of order to demonstrate their skills in arms. The challenger often wore a badge or something similar, such as a garter, and this might also be the chosen prize.

In 1400 Sir John Prendergast accepted a challenge from an Aragonese esquire, Michel d'Oris, but despite letters passing via heralds, the combat came to nothing. John Astley fought a combat at Paris against Piers de Massy on 29 August 1438, watched by King Charles VII. In this episode Astley struck his opponent in the head with his lance, killing him. Astley was challenged in January 1442 by an Aragonese knight, Philip Boyle, and the contest took place at Smithfield. Boyle was slightly wounded; Astley gained the advantage and was about to thrust his dagger into Boyle's face when King Henry VI, who was watching, stopped the combat. The king knighted Astley there and then,

A late 15th-century depiction of a joust of war before Richard II at Smithfield in 1394. The knights wear field armour. In Richard's day the fleurs-de-lis had not yet been reduced to three in each quarter of the shield. (Lambeth Palace Library, MS 6, f.233)

The late 15th-century *Beauchamp Pageant* depicts Sir Richard Beauchamp and Sir Hugh Lawney shattering their blunted lances in a joust of peace in 1414. Sir Hugh wears an armet, the visor of which has been flung up. The manifer on his left arm can be clearly seen, as can the polder-mitten of Sir Richard. (By permission of the British Library, MS Cotton Julius E IV, art. 6, f.15v)

giving him in addition 100 marks a year for life.

In 1465 Anthony Woodville, Lord Scales, brother-in-law to Edward IV, issued a challenge to Anthony, Bastard of Burgundy. Because large-scale affairs were relatively uncommon in England, this event attracted a number of writers. Woodville was probably aping the Burgundian lifestyle. The story goes that the ladies of Edward's court surrounded Woodville and tied a gold band round his thigh, with a 'flower of remembrance' and articles for a joust. Two years later the challenge was accepted. Despite detailed regulations that included the forbidding of spiked horse armour, the Bastard's horse was killed in a collision with his opponent. This aroused suspicion, which Scales was able to refute, though a piece from his sword was apparently found in the dead animal. The resultant foot combat was stopped by the king after a few strokes of the axe gave Scales the advantage, although further combats between English and Burgundian knights took place.

For a knight of quality, appearance at any large spectacle would necessitate a show of wealth on his part, not only in his armour and weapons but also in his horse trappings, the costumes of his attendants and, occasionally, in the largesse he might distribute.

MEDICAL CARE, DEATH AND BURIAL

Knights who were injured or sick faced two obstacles on any road to recovery. Firstly, dependent on their rank, they might or might not get the chance to see a surgeon. Secondly, if they did get medical attention, a great deal depended on the quality of the physician and the nature of the wound.

The king and the great nobles would have surgeons in their pay and such men would travel with their master when they were on the move. Thomas Morestede is styled as the King's Surgeon in his agreement with Henry V for the invasion of France in 1415, where he is also to provide three archers and 12 'hommes de son mestier' (men of his service). In addition, William Bradwardyn is listed as a surgeon and both he and

Morestede came with nine more surgeons each, making a total of 20 for the army.

Some surgeons were retained by indenture in the same way as the soldiers. John Paston, who was hit below the right elbow by an arrow during the battle of Barnet in 1471, managed to escape with other fleeing Yorkists but lost his baggage. His brother sent a surgeon who stayed with him and used his 'leechcraft' and 'physic' until the wound was on the mend, though John complained it cost £5 in a fortnight and he was broke.

The medical care itself was a mixture of skill and luck, since astrology and the doctrine of humours played a large part in medical care. Surgeons of repute were taught at the school of Montpellier in the Languedoc-Rousillon region of southern France, but even these men would have limited skills. Many could treat broken legs or dislocations successfully, even hernias, and carried out amputations, though a lack of knowledge of bacteria made it a risky business for the patient. Some used alcohol, opium or mandragora to dull the pain. Neither instruments nor hands were necessarily washed. Open wounds could be treated by stitching, and egg yolks were recognised as a soothing balm. However, blood was staunched by the use of a hot iron.

Arrows might go deep, though by this time it was less common to be hit by one with a head bearing barbs, especially when wearing armour. Yet arrows were often stuck in the ground for swift reloading, and conveyed on their tips a lethal dose of dirt which, together with cloth fragments, would be carried into the wound. Abdominal wounds were usually fatal, and surgery was fairly lethal, since any tear in the gut would allow material into the abdominal cavity (not to mention dirt from the weapon used), resulting in peritonitis and death. However, skeletons from the battle of Towton in 1461 show that men did survive quite horrendous wounds. Bones show evidence of slashing blows which bit through muscle into the bone itself, in some cases shearing off pieces. One individual in particular had been in battle before, having been struck across the jaw with such force that the blade cut across to the other side of the mouth. He also had wounds to the skull, but survived all of these, with some disfigurement, to face

Sir Richard Beauchamp strikes Sir Colard Fynes in a joust of war with sharp lances. The large reinforce can clearly be seen on Sir Colard's shoulder and left arm. (By permission of the British Library, MS Cotton Julius E IV, art. 6, f.16)

A knight arming for foot combat in the lists, from *How a Man Schall be Armyd*, a manuscript of the later 15th century and the only known medieval portrayal of an arming doublet with mail gussets. The varlet is tying on a mail skirt. The knight's great basinet lies on the table and a pollaxe and an **Ahlespiess** is propped up at the side. (Pierpont Morgan Library, M.775, f.122v)

action once more at Towton, knowing what that might entail – in this instance his own death. Although knights might wear better armour, it was (theoretically) their job to lead from the front. Some unfortunate knights neither escaped nor perished, but were left for dead, robbed and left half-naked in the open unless by chance they were discovered and succoured.

Much of the Towton evidence comes from men who were infantry. Compression of the left arm bones strongly suggests that some were almost certainly longbowmen. They appear to have been killed during the rout or after capture, and some have several wounds, especially to the head, suggesting that once cut down, further blows were delivered to finish them off. Presumably they had no helmet, or had discarded or lost them while being pursued. The victims were then placed in grave pits. Knights and men of rank might escape such a fate. After Agincourt, the Duke of York's body was boiled and the bones brought back to England for burial. Similarly those of lords would be found either by their retainers or else by heralds, whose job it was to wander the field and book the dead (meaning those with coats-of-arms), which gave the victor a good indication of how he had fared. The families would then transport the body back to be buried on home ground, in the case of the nobility next to their ancestors. Otherwise they were buried locally, usually in a churchyard.

During the turmoil of the Wars of the Roses, with men supporting rivals to the throne, treason was an easy and swift charge to bring. For example, after the battle of Wakefield in 1460, Richard Neville, Earl of Salisbury, was captured and executed next day. Men of rank killed whilst in revolt might also undergo the degradation of public humiliation. This was not common during the first part of the century, since much of the time knights fought in France, where they were usually treated as honourable opponents. Warwick the Kingmaker, having been slain at Barnet in 1471, was brought to London and displayed for all to see, before his body was allowed to rest at Bisham Abbey with other family members. Richard III was exposed for two days in the Church of St Mary in the Newarke in Leicester, naked except for a piece of cloth, and then buried in a plain tomb in the house of the Grey Friars nearby. Salisbury's head, with those of the Duke of York and his young son, Earl of Rutland, both killed at Wakefield, was stuck on a spike on the walls of York, the Duke's complete with a paper crown.

Being treated to the indignity of having one's head spiked on London Bridge or on other town gates served as a warning to all those passing beneath. However, a number of attainders[1] were reversed, such as that of Sir Richard Tunstall who, despite being placed in the Tower, managed to persuade Edward IV that he was more use alive and gained his favour. Children of those who died accused of treason did not usually suffer because of it, though their father's lands might pass to the crown until they inherited them.

1 The loss of civil rights following a sentence of death or outlawry for treason or felony

In contrast to this brutality, there is evidence that humanity and regret did exist. Chantry chapels were set up on various battlefields to pray for the souls of those who died, for example at Barnet, some half a mile (800 m) from the town, where the corpses were buried. Richard III endowed Queen's College, Cambridge, for prayers to be said for those of his retinue who perished at Barnet and Tewkesbury. Nobles might make provision for men of their retinues to be cared for if wounded; Henry of Northumberland told his executors to carry out such wishes if he should be killed at Bosworth.

About 30 nobles were killed during the Wars of the Roses, together with numerous knights, those spared being the result of political necessity or on behalf of a family, rather than for any high-minded notions of chivalry. However, other nobles, including men who never fought, survived largely because the Yorkist monarchs, with a narrow band of noble supporters, needed to win Lancastrian support. Despite Edward IV being finally forced to destroy the Beauforts and Henry VI and his son, the Yorkists' years of rule were by no means all of blood. Henry VII and Tudor propagandists would try to maintain this argument in an effort to stabilise the crown and remove bastard feudalism.

Foot combat in the lists, with great basinets much in evidence though outdated on the battlefield. (By permission of the British Library, MS Harley 4375, f.171v)

A tourney or team event during an English tournament in about 1500. Unusually, all the knights wear frog-mouthed helms, which would restrict visibility if sword play was also expected. (By permission of the British Library, MS Harley 326, f.113)

GLOSSARY

Ahlespiess: A staff weapon for thrusting, consisting of a quadrangular-sectioned spike with a **rondel** to guard the hand.

Aketon: A padded coat, usually quilted vertically, which was worn beneath mail to absorb blows.

Aiglet: A conical metal finial attached to the end of a point to prevent fraying and to ease passage through an eyelet.

Alwite: Plate armour that is not faced with material.

Arçons: The **bow** and **cantle** of a saddle.

Armet: An Italian closed helmet with cheek-pieces that opened outwards to allow it to be put on.

Arming cap: A padded and quilted cap, sometimes worn under the helmet and always worn by lesser soldiers if a mail hood was still used.

Arming doublet: A jacket worn beneath plate armour. It had gussets of mail attached to guard exposed parts and **arming points** to attach pieces of armour.

Arming point: A flax, twine or buckskin lace used to attach armour.

Arming sword: The main fighting sword of a knight.

Aventail: Mail neck-defence attached to the lower edge of a **basinet**; smaller versions were attached to **armets**.

Backplate: Plate armour for the back.

Ballock knife: A knife or dagger whose hilt has two swellings at the base next to the blade. Also called a kidney dagger by Victorians.

Banneret: A knight entitled to bring vassals onto the field under his own banner.

Barbut: A deep Italian helmet with a 'T'-shaped face-opening.

Bard: Full plate armour for a horse.

Baselard: A long civilian dagger or short sword, with an 'H'-shaped hilt.

Basinet: A conical open-faced helmet which extended down at the sides and back.

Bastard sword: A sword capable of being wielded in one or both hands.

Bec-de-faucon: An axe or hammer backed by a beak like that of a falcon.

Besagew: Roundel suspended to protect the armpit.

Bevor: Plate throat-defence used in conjunction with a **sallet**.

Bill: A staff weapon derived from a hedging bill, consisting of a broad convex blade with a spike at the top and rear.

Bodkin: A long arrow-head without barbs, for piercing armour.

Bow: The front of the saddle.

Breastplate: Plate armour for the chest and stomach.

Breaths: Holes in a helmet for ventilation and increased vision.

Brigandine: Body armour consisting of a canvas jacket inside which were riveted many small plates. The outside was usually faced with cloth or leather.

Broad-head: A wide barbed arrow-head with long cutting edges, used for hunting or maiming war-horses.

Cannon: Tubular or gutter-shaped plate defence for the upper or lower arm. Also the term for a gun so large that it needed to be supported on a bed or carriage.

Cantle: The rear part of a saddle.

Cap-à-pie: Fully armed, literally 'head to foot'.

Caparison: Cloth, or occasionally mail, covering or housing for a horse, often used to carry the owner's coat-of-arms.

Celata: An open-faced Italian **sallet**.

Chape: A metal terminal fitted over the tip of a scabbard to protect it.

Chevauchée: An armed expedition into enemy territory.

Coat of plates: Body armour consisting of a canvas jacket inside which plates were riveted. The outside was usually faced with cloth or leather; also called 'pair of plates' or 'plates'.

Coronel: A small crown of points used instead of a single sharp head on lances for **jousts of peace**. The use of several points helped spread the impact of the blow.

Courser: A war-horse.

Couter: Plate defence for the elbow.

Crinet: Plate defence for a horse's neck.

Crupper: Plate armour for a horse's rump.

Cuirass: Armour for the torso, usually denoting the breast- and back-plates, **fauld** and **culet**.

Cuir-bouilli: Leather moulded and hardened following suspension in water or boiling.

Cuisse: Plate armour for the thigh.

Culet: Plate defence below the backplate.

Destrier: The largest, strongest and most expensive war-horse.

Dubbing: The tap on the shoulder with a sword that made a man a knight.

Enarmes: Carrying straps fitted inside a shield.

Estoc: A thrusting sword with a long, stiff blade. Also called a **tuck** in England.

Falchion: A cleaver-like single-edged short sword.

Fauld: The hooped skirt that hung from the breastplate to guard the lower abdomen.

Fauchard: A staff weapon consisting of a long cleaver-like blade, with a **rondel** to guard the hand. It was popular with French infantry.

Flanchard: Plate armour for a horse's flank. Rarely used.

Frog-mouthed helm: A **helm** whose lower front plate below the vision slit was extended forward to deflect a blow. Also known as a tilting helm, and used largely for **jousts of peace**.

Gadling: A proud metal stud on the knuckle or finger joint of a **gauntlet**.

Gaignepain: Gauntlet, probably of leather, worn on the right hand with armours for **jousts of peace**.

Gambeson: A padded coat usually quilted vertically. The term generally refers to a coat worn over the armour rather than beneath it.

Gardbrace: A reinforcing plate worn over the **pauldron** on Italian and some west-European armours.

Gauntlet: Defence for the hand and wrist.

Gisarme: Also called **guisarme**. A staff weapon consisting of a convex axe-head with the lowest point attached to the shaft.

Glaive: see **fauchard**.

Gorget: A plate collar to guard the throat.

Graper: A stop behind the grip on a lance.

Great basinet: A **basinet** with plate throat- and neck-defences attached.

Greave: Plate armour for the lower leg.

Guard-of-the-vambrace: A reinforcing plate worn over the front of the **couter** on Italian and some west-European armours.

Guige: The strap for suspending the shield from the neck or for hanging from a peg.

Guisarme: See **gisarme**.

Hackney: A riding horse.

Halberd: A staff weapon consisting of an axe blade backed by a fluke and surmounted by a spike.

Hand-and-a-half sword: See **Bastard sword**.

Haute-piece: An upstanding flange formed by bending up the upper edge of a **pauldron**.

Helm: A large helmet enclosing the entire head which, in the 15th century, was used only in the tournament.

Herald: An official employed by a king or nobleman, and who wore his arms. Heralds delivered messages and identified coats-of-arms.

Hounskull: The name sometimes given to the pointed visor worn with the **basinet**. Such a combination also gave rise to the Victorian term: 'pig-faced' basinet.

Jack: A quilted jacket made from many layers of linen or two layers stuffed with tow.

Jousts of peace: Mounted contest between two opponents using blunted lances.

Jousts of war: Mounted contest between two opponents using sharp lances.

Jupon: Also spelt 'gipoun'. A cloth coat worn over the tunic and buttoned or laced down the front. The term also refers to a similar style of surcoat worn over armour.

Kettle-hat: Open-faced helmet with a broad brim.

King of arms: The rank above that of **herald**.

Klappvisier: A visor attached at the brow of the helmet instead of the sides.

Lame: A strip or plate of steel, sometimes used to provide articulation in armour.

Lance: A long spear used on horseback, now sometimes swelling slightly towards and behind the grip.

Lance-rest: A bracket attached to the wearer's right side of the breastplate to stop a lance running back when a strike is made. It derives from the French word: *Arrête*.

Langet: A metal strip attached to the head of a staff weapon, nailed to the shaft to provide a more secure fixture and to help prevent the wood from being cut.

Latten: Copper-alloy very like brass, used for decorating some plate armour.

Lists: The tournament arena where combats took place.

Livery: Robes worn by a lord's followers, bearing his badge and colours.

Locket: A metal mount to protect the mouth of a scabbard or sheath.

Mail: Armour made from thousands of interlinked iron rings. Most were riveted, but sometimes alternate lines of riveted and welded rings were used.

Manifer: Large plate mitten-gauntlet for the left hand, attached over the ordinary **gauntlet** when worn with armours for **jousts of peace**.

Palfrey: A good riding horse.

Pauldron: Plate shoulder-defence that overlapped the chest and back.

Peytral: Plate, or occasionally mail, defence for a horse's chest.

Pike: A long infantry spear.

Plackart: Plate stomach defence.

Point: A flax, twine or buckskin lace used to attach armour or tie up items of clothing.

Poire: A pear-shaped wooden or leather buffer hung behind the shield on the breastplate of west-European armours for **jousts of peace**.

Polder-mitten: Lower cannon with a large, shell-like plate covering the outside of the elbow, the joint and part of the upper arm, worn on the right arm in **jousts of peace**.

Poleyn: Plate armour for the knee.

Pollaxe: A staff weapon with a spike at the top, and axe blade backed by a hammer. Some examples had a hammer backed by a beak..

Pommel: The weighted end of a sword hilt. The front bow of a saddle

Pursuivant: The rank below that of **herald**, identified by wearing the tabard sideways.

Rebated point: A blunted weapon point, for use in tournament contests.

Rondel: A disc attached to some staff weapons to guard the hand, and behind an **armet** to guard the strap holding the **wrapper**.

Rondel dagger: A dagger with a disc at each end of the hilt to guard the hand.

Rouncy: A horse suitable only for casual riding.

Rump-guard: A single plate that hung from the **culet**.

Sabaton: Plate armour for the foot.

Sallet: A helmet drawn out to a tail at the rear. Some were open-faced, others protected the face.

Shaffron: Plate defence for a horse's head.

Side wing: A plate extending from the **couter** to guard the inside of the elbow or from the **poleyn** to guard the outside of the knee.

Skull: The main part of a helmet. Also a simple metal cap.

Spaudler: Plate shoulder-defence.

Standard: Mail neck-defence, usually with an upstanding collar of mail links.

Stop-rib: A raised strip of steel riveted to a plate to guide weapon-points away.

Sumpter: A pack horse or mule.

Tabard: A loose surcoat, usually open at the sides, which was put on over the head. It had wide elbow-length sleeves, and was used to display the wearer's arms. **Heralds** wore a similar coat with their master's arms.

Tang: The continuation of a sword blade that passed through the hilt.

Tasset: A small plate that hung from the **fauld** as a pair.

Tilt: The barrier separating two contestants in the jousts, usually in **jousts of peace**. Also known as a 'toile', it was originally of cloth but was soon replaced by a wooden barrier.

Tournament: Originally a contest between two teams, but later used to embrace the developed form in which jousting and foot combat also took place.

Tourney: A term used to denote the mounted team event during a tournament, to distinguish it from other events.

Trapper: See **Caparison**.

Tuck: The English name for an **Estoc**.

Vambrace: Plate arm defence.

Vamplate: A circular plate attached over the lance to guard the hand.

War hammer: A horseman's weapon of the late 15th century consisting of a short staff with a hammer-head. The horseman's pick was a form backed by a fluke.

Wrapper: A prow-shaped plate strapped over the lower part of an **armet**.

BIBLIOGRAPHY

Barber, Richard, *The Knight and Chivalry*, Longman Group Ltd (London, 1970)

Barber, Richard, and Barker, Juliet, *Tournaments: Jousts Chivalry and Pageants in the Middle Ages*, The Boydell Press (Woodbridge, 1989)

Bellamy, J. G., *Bastard Feudalism and the Law*, Routledge (London, 1989)

Blair, Claude, *European Armour*, B. T. Batsford Ltd (London, 1958)

Boardman, Andrew W., *The Medieval Soldier in the Wars of the Roses*, Sutton Publishing Ltd (Stroud, 1998)

Boccia, Linello Giorgio, *Le Armature di S. Maria delle Grazie di Curtatone di Mantova e L'Armatura Lombarda del '400*, Bramante Editrice (Busto Arsizio, 1982)

Bradbury, J., *The Medieval Archer*, The Boydell Press (Woodbridge, 1985)

Bradbury, J., *The Medieval Siege*, The Boydell Press (Woodbridge, 1992)

Burgess, E. Martin, 'The Mail-Maker's Technique', *Antiquaries Journal* XXXIII pp. 48–55 (London, 1953)

Burgess, E. Martin, 'Further research into the construction of mail garments', *Antiquaries Journal* XXXIII pp. 193–202 (London, 1953)

Contamine, Philippe, *War in the Middle Ages* (trans Jones, Michael), Basil Blackwell Ltd (Oxford, 1984)

Cunnington, C. Willett and Phillis, *Handbook of English Mediaeval Costume*, Faber & Faber Ltd (London, 1969)

Curry, Anne, and Hughes, Michael, *Arms, Armies and Fortifications in the Hundred Years War*, The Boydell Press (Woodbridge, 1994)

Davis, R. H. C., *The Medieval Warhorse*, Thames & Hudson Ltd (London, 1989)

Dufty, R., and Read, W., *European Armour in the Tower of London*, HMSO (London, 1968)

Edge, David, and Paddock, John Miles, *Arms and Armour of the Medieval Knight*, Bison Books Ltd (London, 1988)

Embleton, Gerry, and Howe, John, *The Medieval Soldier*, Windrow & Greene Ltd (London, 1994)

Fiorato, Veronica, Boylton, Anthea and Knüsel, Christopher, *Blood Red Roses*, Oxbow Books (Oxford, 2000)

Foss, Michael, *Chivalry*, Michael Joseph Ltd (London, 1975)

Gies, Frances, *The Knight in History*, Robert Hale Ltd (London, 1986)

Gravett, Christopher and Breckon, Brett, *The World of the Medieval Knight*, MacDonald Young Books (Hove, 1996)

Haigh, P. A., *The Military Campaigns of the Wars of the Roses*, Sutton Publishing Ltd (Stroud, 1995)

Keegan, J., *The Face of Battle*, Pimlico (1991)

Keen, Maurice, *Chivalry*, Yale University Press (London, 1984)

Koch, H. W., *Medieval Warfare*, Bison Books Ltd (London, 1978)

Lander, J. R., *The Wars of the Roses*, Secker & Warburg (London, 1965)

Mann, Sir James, *Wallace Collection Catalogues. European Arms and Armour*, 2 vols., The Trustees of the Wallace Collection (London, 1962)

Myers, R. A., *The Household of Edward IV*, Manchester University Press (Manchester, 1959)

Nicolas, Sir Harris, *Wardrobe Accounts of Edward IV*, W. Pickering (London, 1830)

Nicolas, Sir Harris, *The History of the Battle of Agincourt* (Facsimile of 1833 edition), H. Pordes (London, 1971)

Norman, A. V. B., *Wallace Collection Catalogues. European Arms and Armour Supplement.* (London, 1986)

Norman A. V. B. and Pottinger, Don, *English Weapons and Warfare 449–1660*, Arms & Armour Press (London, 1979)

Oakeshott, R. Ewart, *The Sword in the Age of Chivalry*, Lutterworth Press (London, 1964)

Pfaffenbichler, Matthias, *Armourers*, British Museum Press (London, 1992)

Prestwich, M., *Armies and Warfare in the Middle Ages*, Yale University Press (London, 1996)

Rudorff, Raymond, *The Knights and their World*, Cassell & Co. Ltd (London, 1974)

Thompson, M. W., *The Decline of the Castle*, Cambridge University Press (Cambridge, 1987)

Turnbull, Stephen, *The Book of the Medieval Knight*, Arms & Armour Press (London, 1985)

THE PLATES

A: THE BATTLE OF AGINCOURT, 25 OCTOBER 1415

Cavalry charges by French men-at-arms on either wing having been defeated by English longbowmen, the French advance their first line of dismounted men-at-arms. This plate depicts the struggle that followed, both sides fighting on foot. A dead French warhorse, despite a steel shaffron to protect his head, sprouts an arrow shaft which shows the depth these missiles penetrated when they struck flesh. A bodkin-headed arrow has bored into the breastplate of a French knight; even steel armour was not always effective against them. Some knights still wear a jupon over their armour but many have discarded it, revealing the smooth steel surfaces. The knight on the left wears a breastplate and fauld attached to a red velvet covering. The older, pointed visor is in evidence alongside the newer, more rounded variety. Similarly, though many still use a basinet with attached mail aventail, others have a great basinet with its plate neck defences. The knightly shield is now disappearing though some horsemen still carry them. Swords are used to hack at lightly armoured archers but only the points are useful against fully armoured knights, when an armpit is exposed or a visor is lifted. Increasingly in evidence were percussion weapons: maces, hammers and staff weapons such as long axes, that could be swung in two hands to deliver a powerful blow.

B: KNIGHT, C.1425

The evidence for armour at this period comes largely from brasses, effigies and manuscript illuminations, since very little survives. **Besagews** at the armpits were very popular. The **basinet** with mail **aventail** would remain a common sight until about 1430, but this knight has a great basinet, used from about 1420 until mid-century. It is quite large and less closely shaped to the head than German versions, here decorated with a jewelled scarf or orle. He wears an arming sword.

1 Great basinet, with bevor and gorget plate.
2 Detached visor, secured by a pin each side.
3 Lancastrian SS collar.
4 Jewelled hip belt with rondel dagger; arming sword with fish-tail pommel suspended from diagonal belt.
5 Arming sword associated with the tomb of Henry V.
6 **Gauntlet**.
7 Rowel spur found at the battlefield of Towton (1461) but of a form common at least 25 years earlier. Until about 1450 some spurs were fastened using a single loop terminal on each arm to attach the hook of the strap terminals. Most, however, were attached using a pair of holes on each arm to which the leathers were fastened above and below the foot.
8 Illustrated are three versions of the houppelande (gown). The cote-hardie (jacket), belted at the hips, was often worn over the doublet and until 1410 it barely reached the fork but then lengthened to the knees. It eventually blended with the short houppelande. It consisted of four pieces seamed at front, rear and sides, which until 1440 might be left open a short distance from the hem to form vents. It was closed by buttons or more often hooks and eyes, usually hidden under the folds. It was frequently lined with

A tourney with blunt swords and a form of great basinet, from the *Beauchamp Pageant*. The Earl of Warwick's crest of a bear and ragged staff can be seen on the left. (By permission of the British Library, MS Cotton Julius E IV, art VI, f.7v)

satin, silk, taffeta, linen or cloth, with fur or cloth for winter versions. The neck, hem, vents and wrists might be furred with sable, ermine (only royalty had the black tails), civet, beaver, grise, fox and lamb. This knee-length houppelande has hanging sleeves. Some hanging sleeves had a slit down the front for the arm to pass through. The bowl crop appeared in 1410 as an extremely popular hair style. Pointed or forked beards were occasionally seen until about 1415.

9 Very short houppelande with high collar and baggy closed sleeves of 'bagpipe' form (with large pouch or 'pokys'), popular until the 1430s. The chaperon was a ready-made hood-turban, from 1420.
10 Houppelande with huge open funnel-shaped sleeves of the type only worn for ceremonial use after about 1420. A padded doublet was worn over the shirt, with holes for the hose. Often called a 'paltock', it was made in eight pieces with a central seam down the back and round the waist. Others might be worn without holes. The quilting was usually horizontal or confined to the lining for civil use, but vertical for military use. Broadcloth, linen, fustian or sometimes leather was used, with damask, silk or velvet for the rich or for ceremonial use. The doublet was rarely uncovered after 1412. A cloak or a shoulder cape ('huke') might be worn, being shorter for riding.

C: CONFRONTATION ON THE ROAD, 22 MAY 1448

Sir Humphrey Stafford, his eldest son, Richard, and their retinue were riding towards their inn at Coventry when they saw Sir Robert Harcourt and his men coming towards them. Harcourt passed Sir Humphrey but when he met Richard the two started arguing. Harcourt then drew his sword and caught the other a glancing blow to the head, but Richard managed to draw his dagger. As he lunged at Harcourt he stumbled and was fatally stabbed in the back by one of Harcourt's men. Sir Humphrey rode back but he too was wounded from behind and fell. His men now attacked and managed to kill two of Harcourt's followers. Next day Harcourt was indicted as principal in the murder of Richard Stafford by the city coroners and arrested. Partly by his own efforts he evaded trial, so on 1 May 1450 Sir Humphrey gathered about 200 men and approached Stanton Harcourt in Oxfordshire by night. He probably knew that the Duke of Suffolk had been murdered, who well might have supported Harcourt in law and in strength. Now Harcourt locked himself in the church tower and staved off all attacks, even the burning of the room under the tower. Harcourt was pardoned, while Sir Humphrey was killed in a fight with Kentish rebels in June. However, Sir Humphrey's bastard son killed Harcourt in 1469.

D: AT THE KINGMAKER'S COURT, 1465

Richard Neville, Earl of Warwick, plots with friends while his one-time ally, Edward IV, talks with his in-laws, the Woodvilles. Courtiers wear dress that befits their rank, and is a conscious statement of their power and wealth. Civilian dress has changed in some ways from the early part of the century. The Earl wears a long black gown (as the houppelande was now called), which often now had vents. It was fastened down the front with hooks and eyes or was double-breasted. He carries a fashionable three-tasselled 'gypcière' at his belt and wears a felt Turkey bonnet, popular from 1450 to 1485. Warwick's followers wear his badge of the ragged staff. The hose had reached the hips by mid-century, and the doublet was fastened by laces, buttons, ties or hooks and eyes. A petticoat or waistcoat (with or without tight sleeves) might be worn between the shirt and doublet, for warmth. The two figures in the foreground wear jackets

Richard Pynson's woodcut of Chaucer's Squire, c.1491. He wears fashionable civilian clothes and long 'piked' riding boots. (By permission of the British Library, MS G.11586 – p.7)

over their doublets. Evolved from the cote-hardie, they sometimes had side vents and might have vertical folds. The right-hand figure has hanging sleeves, and both wear long pointed (piked) shoes. The bowl crop lengthened from about 1450–75, but already in 1465 a 'page-boy' style with fringe and long hair sometimes to the shoulders, was becoming popular and would remain so. Beards were rare. Youths still used folly bells; short riding hukes had almost disappeared.

E: ITALIAN ARMOUR, C.1450

The main picture is based on the Milanese harness now in the Scott Collection in Glasgow, with its missing pieces restored and the **barbut** replaced by an **armet**. The breast hinges to the back on the wearer's left (with removable pins) and is strapped on the right; this keeps vulnerable straps away from the side which was most commonly presented to an opponent. The **fauld** is held on internal leathers, straps which act to join plates together while allowing them some movement. Beneath, a mail skirt is tied around the waist to allow movement while protecting the genitals. For combat on foot this might be replaced by mail pants. The lance-rest on the breastplate is held by a staple and pin. Mail **sabatons** were common in Italy, being attached to a line of holes on the lower edge of the greave.

1 The armet opened; it is fitted with a padded lining of hay, wool or tow, stitched to a lining-band riveted inside. A mail **aventail** would be attached to a leather strip pierced with holes that fit over staples along the lower edge of the armet, and is secured by a cord passed through the staples.
2 The visor is removed by withdrawing a pin at each side.
3 A **wrapper** can be strapped over the visor and cheek-pieces. Edges are turned outwards over wire to remove sharp metal.
4 A stop-rib is riveted to the main plate of the **pauldron**; the plates above articulate on pivoting rivets.
5 A **gardbrace** attaches to each pauldron by a staple and pin, the left being much larger.
6 The **lames** of the **couter** attach on pivoting rivets, to prevent gaps appearing when the arm is bent. The lower cannon is attached to the lower couter plate by a sliding rivet (moving in a slot), allowing the forearm to twist slightly.
7 The large guard of the **vambrace** – characteristically Italian in its size – fits over the left couter wing via a staple and pin.
8 The **gauntlet** has a leather glove stitched to a canvas or leather lining-band riveted inside the cuff and secured at the hand by rivets and straps. Each exposed finger end additionally has a leather strip stitched to it, on to which are riveted overlapping steel scales. The left gauntlet has one plate over the fingers, the right, which requires more flexibility for gripping weapons, has two.
9 The **cuisse** has a leather tongue pierced with holes to attach to the doublet. The **poleyn**, with large Italian side wing, has **lames** above and below that allow the leg to bend without exposing the limb itself. The **greave** is strapped on the inner side of the leg.
10 An Italian **sallet**, c.1450.
11 Italian **sallet** covered in velvet and decorated with gilt copper mounts, c. 1480

F: ENGLISH ARMOUR, 1450–1500

Examples of the west European armour worn in England are

A late 15th-century composite South German 'Gothic' armour, mounted on a horse armour made at Augsburg in about 1480, probably for Waldemar VI of Anhalt-Zerbst. The German armour is visually quite different, being long and fluted while the Italian is rounded and smooth. Sabatons are worn on the feet. The arm-defence shown here is joined as one, but often it comprised separate lower and upper cannons and couter. The plackart is riveted to the breast instead of being strapped on, the lance-rest riveted in place instead of having a staple. A sallet and bevor is worn. English lords might have worn armours such as this very occasionally, though there is little evidence. (By courtesy of the Trustees of the Armouries, II.3, VI.379)

rare and we are thrown back on visual evidence to reconstruct it. The example illustrated may have been made in England, probably London, or else imported from Flanders. Some armour might be of Italian export type, made in the style required in England. The knight carrying the pollaxe is based on the FitzHerbert effigy, of *c*.1475. Much of the detail mentioned in the description of Italian armour on Plate E applies to the western Europe form, including the articulation of plates. English armour is also much like Italian armour in style but with a number of variations. **Sabatons** of overlapping **lames**, each joined by a pivoting rivet, were commonly used rather than mail over the foot. A strap under the foot acts as a stirrup, and some were tied through the toe-piece with **points**. The wing on the **poleyn** was not as

large as on Italian examples, and was heart-shaped. The **plackart** was often attached to the breastplate by a rivet rather than a strap. **Besagews** were still sometimes worn, though they are not shown here. The left and right wings of the **couters** were more likely to be symmetrical. The **vambrace** was often made in three parts in the fashion popular in Germany. The German influence upon this example is clear from the points visible on the couter and which were used to secure it over the arming doublet.

Gauntlets were laminated at the wrist, and some had several lames over part of the fingers on both hands. A reinforcing plate might be strapped to the left hand. The armour is often fluted and cusped to some extent. After about 1470 the **tassets** are strapped on halfway up the **fauld**, instead of hanging from the edge. By about 1440 the English knight's helmet was likely to have been a **sallet**, of a more upright form than in Germany.

1 **Sallet**, *c*. 1460, showing lining of canvas stuffed with hay. Stitched to a canvas or leather band held by rivets visible on the outside, the lining was cut into sections conected at the top by a draw string. This made the helmet fit the head in the same way each time, aligning the vision slits with the eyes.
2 A lined **bevor**, laced or stapled to the breastplate, was not always worn with the sallet. **Armets** were not very common, nor was the **barbut**.
3 Yorkist collar with lion pendant.
4 Boar pendant of Richard of Gloucester. The Duke of York gave Sir John Fastolf a white rose collar, which included a diamond set in a rose, valued at 4,000 marks.
5 **War-hammer** *c*. 1450.
6 Flanged mace *c*. 1470.
7 Hand-and-a-half sword with scent-bottle pommel, *c*.1450. The leather flap below the hilt fits over the scabbard mouth to help stop water entering it. A membrane of leather is fitted over the cord binding.
8 Arming sword with fish-tail pommel, second half of the 15th century.
9 Exploded view of the hilt, showing the wooden carved core pierced to receive the tang, mid-15th century. The wood was usually covered in leather and perhaps overlaid with cloth or leather strips, or wire
10 Hand-and-a-half sword with scent-bottle pommel, *c*.1450. The lower half of the grip is additionally covered with leather.
11 Hilt with scent-bottle pommel inset with enamel shield, late-15th century
12 Short, broad-bladed arming sword and scabbard, from the effigy of Sir Robert Harcourt (died 1471). Scabbards were made of wooden boards covered in leather, often highly decorated. It is supported by a typical bifurcated strap arrangement of the period.

G: EQUIPMENT, 2ND HALF OF THE 15TH CENTURY

This knight wears a **brigandine** over mail skirt and sleeves, together with plate armour on the limbs. He carries a **glaive**.

1 The brigandine was made from a canvas jacket, which was lined with small plates secured by rivets through the front. Sometimes two large addorsed 'L'-shaped internal plates (less commonly, one) covered the chest. A smaller version, sometimes with backplate, was popular from

mid-century. The brigandine was usually faced with leather, fustian, velvet, silk, satin or cloth of gold. Rivets might also be set in horizontal lines, the heads tinned or of gilt **latten**. Laces sometimes replaced straps, and late examples sometimes fastened at the sides instead.

2 Upstanding mail collar, made from thicker rings for stiffness.

3 Linen drawers possibly with cod; some may have had a slit instead.

4 Doublet and hose, 1450. The hose had reached the hips and were pointed to the doublet. Stirrups are worn, though footed hose were more usual.

5 Doublet and hose, late 15th century. The hose now reached the waist, still pointed to the doublet. The puffed shoulders (*mahoitres*) were a Burgundian fashion.

6 **Rondel daggers**.

7 **Ballock dagger** or knife, with two swellings at the base of the hilt, often worn with civilian dress.

8 Dagger.

9 **Ahlespiess**.

10 War saddles consisted of a wooden tree, the **arçons** sometimes reinforced by 'steels' screwed to the front and rear faces. Long **trappers** appear to have become less common as the century progressed, but they remained popular for use in the tournament.

11 Stirrup of later 15th century form. Stirrups were often asymmetrical, with broad sides and footrest, the suspension-loop so/metimes masked by a plate. At the beginning of the century a small triangular tongue was often added in the centre of the foot-plate. As the century progresses stirrups become increasingly solid in form.

12 Rowel spurs increased in length as the century went on, only shortening again suddenly in about 1500. One form developed a deeper body during the first half of the century. In the second half a less angular body was used, typically with the longer shank.

H: TOURNAMENT ARMOUR

The first reference to specialised armours for the popular jousts of peace with blunted lances comes in the reign of Edward IV. Prior to this, combatants basically wore field armour with a frog-mouthed **helm** and some reinforces, after about 1430 usually with a tilt or barrier. A French description of 1446 describes specialised armour for such courses, which, by comparing with later Flemish armours, allows a reconstruction of a later 15th-century harness.

1 A frog-mouthed helm is worn which, says the French manuscript, has buckles for the helm and other pieces. Later helms might have had hasps and staples, or screws. Most helms had holes and slits through which points and straps for securing a lining passed. They also usually had ventilation holes on the right side, away from any chance of catching a lance head. Some, as here, even had large openings on the right, occasionally with a trapdoor. Sometimes an **armet** with frog-mouthed visor appears to have been used, and some late 15th-century helms may have had a removable visor, allowing the helmet to be adapted for foot combat as in 16th-century examples. In about 1500 a small group of English helms were of the squat 'pill box' variety. A large **manifer** was worn over the

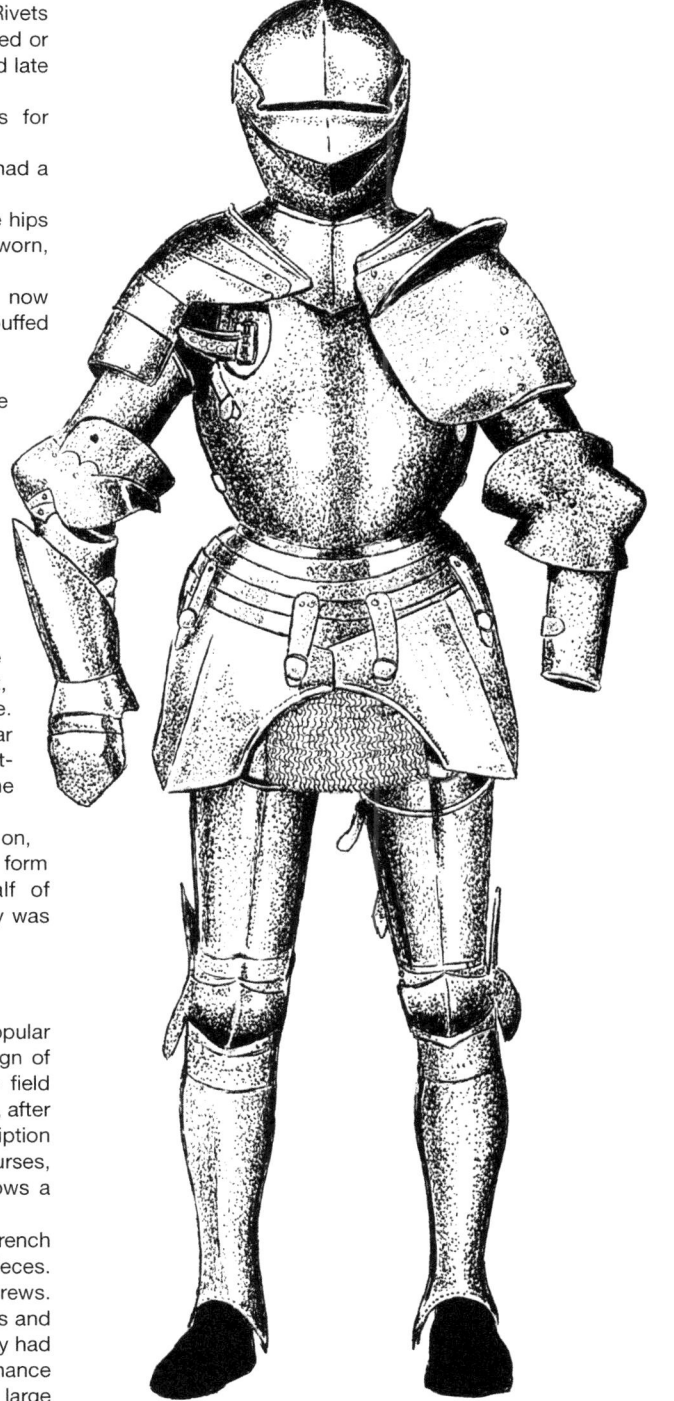

An Italian armour of about 1490 from the Sanctuario Maria delle Grazie, Mantua. The couters have now reduced in size, and in about 1500 the main plate of the cuisse would curve up to follow the plate above it. The visor pivots are now hidden behind the extended arms.

A great basinet for the tourney with blunt swords,
c. 1490–1500, from the church at Wimborne Minster, Dorset.
(By courtesy of the Parish Council and the Trustees of the
Armouries, AI)

gauntlet on the left arm; on some Flemish armours this is
supported by a cord running through a staple on the
breastplate or **brigandine**. A small **gaignepain** or glove
(probably of leather) was worn on the right hand. A thick
shield sometimes faced with small horn squares was laced
to a staple on the breastplate by a cord passing through
holes in the wood. The shield was buffered at the back by
a wooden or leather **poire** (so-called because it was
shaped like a pear) stapled to the breastplate. The
manuscript describes a small one-piece **pauldron** on the
left shoulder, on the right a small laminated pauldron fitted
with a besagew. The bend of the right arm was guarded by
a **polder-mitten**, a lower cannon with a large plate
extending upwards. In England some jousts of peace were
run with leg armour.

2 The helm for jousts of peace, associated with Henry V.
3 High saddle for jousts of peace. Made from wood covered
in leather, it raises the jouster several inches off the horse'
back. The long front extensions also guard the rider's legs,
so that in some jousts leg armour was discarded.
4 Lance with **coronel** head for jousts of peace. A metal
graper is fitted behind the hand, whose points bit into a
piece of wood sitting in a special lance-rest. A **vamplate**
protects the hand.
5 Sharp head for jousts of war. Such jousts were usually run
in field armour, often with armet and **wrapper**. A
'grandguard' covering the left shoulder and chest, and
'pasguard' for the left elbow, appeared in mid-century. For

jousts 'at large' or 'at random' (without a barrier) these
pieces were removed after shattering the lances when
swords came into play. Similar armour was often worn for
the tourney or mounted team event. The central figure is
dressed for the club **tourney**, with a brigandine, though a
cuirass could be worn, plus a great **basinet**.
6 Great basinet from Wimborne Minster in Dorset,
1490–1500. Such helmets could also be used for foot
combat. Field armour fitted with a great basinet strapped,
or latterly double-stapled to the breastplate and strapped
to the backplate with a double buckle, was usually
employed for such contests. A variety of weapons were
used, though the **pollaxe** was common.

I: THE BATTLE OF WAKEFIELD, 31 DECEMBER 1460

Richard, Duke of York, having brought an army north against
the newly raised forces of Henry VI's queen, Margaret of
Anjou, spent Christmas at Sandal Castle. Five days later the
larger Lancastrian army appeared. Reluctant to risk
desertions during a siege, and wary of relief forces, they held
part of their army in a wood whilst the rest lured York's men
out. Archers opened the fighting, and when the Yorkists were
far enough out, the Lancastrians stood and clashed with
their enemies. The second division then appeared and the
Yorkists were doomed. The Duke, shown in an Italian
armour with tabard over it, was killed. His young son, the
Earl of Rutland, caught fleeing by Lord Clifford, was
personally stabbed by him with the words (according to the
16th-century chronicler, Hall): 'Thy father slew mine and so
will I do thee and all thy kin'. The old Earl of Salisbury was
caught and executed next day.

Some knights wear heraldic tabards; one has his armour
painted black, thought to protect it from rust. The knight on
the far right wears a **brigandine** and a form of **sallet**, whose
lower edge reached further down than the visor. By about
1450 these had become level, and the tail had slightly
lengthened. Lying in the foreground a retainer in his lord's
livery wears a **jack**, a padded coat usually made from
numerous layers of linen, or else of two layers stuffed with
tow, and quilted. Sir John Fastolf's inventory of 1459 shows
that he owned one of black linen stuffed with mail and six
others stuffed with horn, as well as 24 caps stuffed with horn
and mail, and six pairs of sheep-skin gloves with mail.

J: THE CONSEQUENCES OF DEFEAT

Not all knights were well treated when they found themselves
on the losing side. At the Battle of Tewkesbury on 4 May
1471, Edward IV, with his brother Gloucester on his left and
Hastings on his right, faced the Lancastrian army of Edmund
Beaufort, Duke of Somerset. With Wenlock and Devon on his
left, he was lining a ridge in front of Tewkesbury town. A
barrage of artillery and arrows poured into Somerset's
forces. Leaving a screen, he led much of his division off to a
hidden road to attack Gloucester's flank. However, the plan
misfired and he arrived at the junction of the divisions of
Gloucester and Edward. Had he been supported by Lord
Wenlock he might have retrieved the situation, but help was
not forthcoming and Edward routed his enemy after he was
aided by 200 spearmen whom he had placed as a flank
guard, and by Gloucester's men.

Struggling to regain the ridge, and infuriated with Wenlock's recalcitrance, Somerset is said to have smashed his mace into the latter's skull, killing him. The Yorkist advance broke the rest of the Lancastrian forces. The Prince of Wales, Henry VI's son, was killed, and men fled in all directions, some through the town and some to the abbey. Here sheltered the Duke of Somerset, Sir John Langstrother, Sir Thomas Tresham and others. It was said that the abbey did not hold a franchise as a sanctuary. One story tells how Edward and a group of men raged through the abbey, killing as traitors many of those they found. Another story says he pardoned them. If the latter is true, the trials of Somerset and other nobles in the presence of Gloucester and Norfolk two days later, and their summary execution in the market place of Tewkesbury, speaks volumes for the callousness present in these wars.

Condemned men were often stripped to their linen shirts;

Relatives search among the dead after a battle. This later 15th-century picture depicts the aftermath at Hastings in 1066. (By permission of the British Library, MS Yates-Thompson 33, f.167)

some of these had a narrow neck-opening with a slit down in front, closed by tying the tails of a tape stitched round the neck opening. The prisoner on the left wears no shirt under his arming doublet and has retained the latter. The gussets of mail under the arm and side to cover weak spots in full plate armour can be seen. Also visible are the arming points hanging from the shoulder, upper arm, elbow and hip, and the points around the hem for securing the hose. There is only one useful picture of a medieval arming doublet, which itself is not highly detailed.

INDEX

Figures in **bold** refer to illustrations

Printed and bound by CPI Group (UK) Ltd, Croydon, CR0 4YY

21/05/2025

01879041-0012